Information Security
A Source Book for Librarians

Information Security
A Source Book for Librarians

C. R. Ramamurthy

AUTHORSPRESS

First Published 2001
by Authorspress

E-35/103, Jawahar Park,
Laxmi Nagar, Delhi-110 092

e-mail: authorspress@yahoo.com
quantum_soul@mantramail.com

Typeset in NewCenturySchlbk by Chitra Computers

Information Security: A Source Book for Librarians
ISBN 81-7273-077-2

Printed in India at Tarun Offset Press, Delhi.

Preface

Rapid advances in information processing, storage and communication technologies have revolutionised the role of worldwide libraries in disseminating information services to their users. Libraries are reconsolidating their positions redesigning their services and information products, incoperating new technologies, upgrading information resources, training people, changing information objects, modes of communication and information delivery in order to add value to their services and to satisfy the changing information needs of user community. As a result libraries are facing new competitors, new demands, new expectations and new security challenges.

Modern technology does not merely promise to create or improve better sensors and alarms to protect library collections. Emergent technology may actually slam the door on potential criminals, rendering them incapable of achieving their goals while helping publicise thefts and alerting other libraries. Today, global libraries use network security policies to ensure the implementation of their security model, in maintaining network security, protection of information loss, alteration, unavailability, and the safeguarding of the organisation's network from internal and external threats. These implementations have often been neglected by users within an organisation, due to their misunderstandings, lack in responsibilities and involvement towards information security in the organisation. For this reason a security awareness policy was developed to ensure that all users involve in a computerised environment, to be on the lookout for any security risks that might occur. This awareness reduces the likelihood for threats from happening, and involves the user to take corrective steps if risks are being identified.

In the future, information security will become a field ripe for experimentation. Assuming that the goal of library provision will still be access to information, it makes sense to seek to improve security at the same time as we strive to enhance and maintain free access.

The present work attempts to provide an authoritative knowledge on diverse aspects of information security and safety in modern libraries. It will serve as a highly informative source book for librarians, info-tech professionals, policy-makers, academicians, teachers, students and so on.

C. R. Ramamurthy

Contents

1
Introduction

Today's changing scenario in the publishing and information technology fields have forced library and information professionals to accept the changing demands placed on the profession today. There is a marked shift from the need of information in academics quality to industry and business houses today. The nature of writing has shifted from single discipline to multi-diciplinary subjects. The value of using management techniques for continuous improvement in quality and reliability has forced us to take a serious view on how libraries and information centres the world over have to reorganise to meet the new challenges of the information technology, publication industry as well as the user demands.

Modern libraries have various methods and technologies to preserve and use the book, namely, acquisition, classification, cataloguing, accessioning, etc. These are treated as library technical activities and once the book is processed through library it is then ready for circulation to users. Though computerisation has eased our operation considerably one cannot say that it has achieved any marked transformation in handling the information as users continue to search their library, and those in the vicinity, with outdated tools. Since there is no interactive activity flow it is obvious that there is a lot of process repetition in libraries all over the country and the world.

Today, in the context of internet, digitisation of information is the key to re-engineer the information management process.

Digitisation means the availability of information in the machine-readable or software form. With such advances in the information technology areas we have now been forced to think again in the new technology phase. Today every large library has a cataloguer whose sole responsibility is to get the output in standard catalogue formats, on catalogue cards. With the above tool the only work that needs to be done is downloading and printing which can be handled by the clerks/typists, thus saving the professional's valuable time and freeing the librarian to do more value-added service to the users.

The development and management of the new information tools will bring about radical-change in the information management. The changes will reduce duplication of work, stop repetitive tasks, release professional time, and have a very highly standardised and generic method of library operations. This in the long run will give rise to a total quality output. With reference to the acquisition process described earlier, re-engineering the whole process will enable one to browse through the internet. Here one can browse through the latest books available, one can read its abstract and scan the contents pages, see the cover page, etc., and then make a decision to purchase.

In libraries the acquisition process is very long drawn out as there are too many intermediary interfaces, e.g., user, vendor, publisher, etc. All these can be eliminated when authorised persons give their recommendations to library to a purchase the book after browsing them on the internet. That alone is not enough, let us imagine that the book is available in its entirety on the net, then purchasing becomes that much simpler thus cutting down the purchase time to a maximum of one hour and also simultaneously overcoming delays caused by geographical boundaries.

Libraries may also order the hard-copy of the book alternately which too could be sent in a couple of weeks time. Apart from saving in time the above gives us information access which is current and available on the net instantly. Check the next scene where the library server is networked within a campus locally through a LAN, and geographically within the country through satellite networks. This would further reduce the research time of looking for books from other libraries.

Inter-library loan of books could be handled electronically, where the whole book can be electronically sent to the requester. The issue of copyright may come up with the publisher which too could be handled by numerous methods—pay when you use or pay when you transmit, etc. Thus re-engineering library and information management, if handled successfully, would open up new avenues to the user, be it a single user or those affiliated to libraries, or corporates.

The term 'information warfare' conjures up a vision of unseen enemies, armed only with laptop personal computers connected to the global computer network, launching untraceable electronic attacks. The digital information that constitutes the national treasury is looted electronically, telephones stop ringing, and emergency services become unresponsive. Although the media are full of scary-sounding stories about violated military websites and broken security on public and corporate networks, the menacing scenarios have remained just that.

Information warfare may be the hep topic of the moment, but a factually solid knowledge of it remains elusive. Hoaxes and myths about information warfare contaminate everything from official reports to newspaper stories. The private sector will not disclose much information about any potential vulnerabilities, even confidentially to the government. Most of the people who know something about the subject are on the government payroll or in the business of selling computer security devices and in no position to serve as objective sources.

The info-war and computer security contain everything from newspaper stories to official reports. Media accounts are so distorted or error-ridden that they are useless as a barometer of the problem. The result has been predictable: confusion over what is real and what is not. Hoaxes about computer viruses have propagated much more successfully than the real things. The myths reach into every corner of modern computing society, and no one is immune. Even those we take to be authoritative on the subject can be unreliable.

A computer virus is a very small programme designed to spread by attaching itself to other bits of executable programme code, which act as hosts for it. The host code can be office applications, utility programmes, games, or special documents created by Microsoft Word that contain embedded computer instructions called macro commands—but not standard text electronic mail. Virus writers have been avidly thinking about this mythical capability for years, and many viruses have been written with malicious intent.

Most attempts to make viruses for use as directed weapons fail for easily understandable reasons. First, it is almost impossible for even the most expert virus writer to anticipate the sheer complexity and heterogeneity of systems the virus will encounter. Second, simple human error is always present. It is an unpleasant fact of life that all software, no matter how well-behaved, harbours errors often unnoticed by its authors.

It is still possible to posit a small team of dedicated professionals employed by a military organisation that could achieve far more success than some alienated teen hackers. But assembling such a team would not be easy. Even though it is not that difficult for those with basic programming skills to write malicious software, writing a really sophisticated computer virus requires some intimate knowledge of the operating system that it is written to work within and the hardware it will be expected to encounter.

Our virus-writing team leader would have to come to grips with the reality, if he is working in the free world, that the pay for productive work in the private sector is a lot more attractive than anything he can offer. Motivation—in terms of remuneration, professional satisfaction, and the recognition that one is actually making something other people can use—would be a big problem for any virus-writing effort attempting to operate in a professional or military setting. Another factor the virus developer would need to consider is that there are no schools turning out information technology professionals who have been trained in virus writing. It is not a course one can take at an engineering school.

In an era of smart bombs, computer viruses are hardly precision-guided munitions. Those that spread do so unpredictably and are as likely to infect the computers of friends and allies as enemies. With militaries around the world using commercial off-the-shelf technology, there simply is no haven safe from potential blow-back by one's creation. Any military commander envisioning the use of computer viruses would have to plan for a reaction by the international antivirus industry, which is well positioned after years of development to provide an antidote to any emerging computer virus.

Computer viruses must be able to spread unnoticeably. Those that do have payloads that go off with a bang or cause poor performance on an infected system get noticed and immediately eliminated. Our virus-writing pros would have to spend a lot of time on intelligence, gaining intimate knowledge of the targeted systems and the ways in which they are used, so their viruses could be written to be maximally compatible. To get that kind of information, the team would need an insider or insiders.

Issues related to electronic commerce and information security are of deep concern to the public, government, researchers, and users of the rapidly expanding internet. The sometimes heated and wide-ranging debate concerning cryptographic policy, content controls, commerce, and interoperability on the internet tends to divert attention away from the need for a reasoned assessment and understanding of the true dynamics of nurturing a diverse global marketplace on the internet.

In the guise of enhanced security and advanced features, proprietary systems and partitioned markets lead to a lack of interoperability that further compromises prospects for society to realise the aforementioned benefits. Many of these problems can be avoided by an open policy-making process that is informed by collaborative research and development activities. It would be ironic indeed if the set of federal policies that founded and sustained the precursors of the evolving electronic marketplace centred on the internet forced those new opportunities offshore. Aside from affecting the balance of trade, jobs and opportunities for further innovation will possibly be lost to overseas competitors.

The information security policies of the cold war era, which provided much of the motivation for the critical federal research and development support of the internet and its predecessors, the NSFnet and ARPANET, threaten to cripple the development of commercially acceptable levels of security for electronic marketplace transactions.

New applications, new users, and faster connections have spurred the internet to become an important medium for communication and information dissemination. Nevertheless, planned and current security policy regarding the internet is not well developed. In its absence entrepreneurs, venture capitalists, technologists, and other nations are amassing knowledge and funding so as to exploit the benefits of the new age.

Complete lack of involvement in this realm would be felt by the lack of a cohesive national policy, the disadvantage our corporations would face in competing against large foreign conglomerates, and an alarming disarray of protocols that do no interoperate, become static, and ultimately fail. However, a partial and misguided federal involvement could be even worse, purposefully crippling the capabilities of our technological sector to meet the worldwide demand for secure and inter-operable communications and commerce.

The growth and benefits of the internet are explained by a combination of economic, technical, and policy factors: positive economic network externalities such as the bandwagon effect, economies of distribution and scale, and statistical sharing; other benefits are the inter-operable and layered approach of the internet, and the distributed peer-to-peer architecture.

Information security does not tend to exhibit positive network effects; instead, it takes an immense amount of knowledge, foresight, and technical skill to design an effective infrastructure. However, the giddy expectations of the internet's abundant information resources and new market potential cannot be fully realised until the alarm over the lack of a security policy expressed by some agencies, businesses, and the public has been addressed.

Library security has always been a problem, although in the past it was somewhat less problematic than it is now. In the Middle Ages, security, inventory, and bibliographic control were not nearly as difficult as they are today, due to several factors. In the Middle Ages, priests and monks, not satisfied with their attempts to keep quick-fingered thieves from stealing by chaining books, imposed even more horrible curses of doom on anyone who stole a book. Perhaps the most effective means ever devised of keeping patrons honest was a simple but eloquent old-fashioned curse, invoking divine wrath, which often acted as an effective deterrent to those inclined to larcenous behaviour.

Throughout the history of civilisation, people have attempted to protect their ownership of books in various ways. Stealing library books and other materials has always cut across social lines. From available evidence, library book thieves throughout recorded history have included high-ranking officials and church elders as well as librarians themselves. More recently, some notorious book thieves have fed off libraries to the tune of thousands of stolen books each.

Much of the literature of security in libraries deals with suggested and recommended counter-measures used to catch these systematic and resourceful felons while preventing other would-be book thieves from following in their footsteps.

The major factors contributing to library theft, violence, and other crime are:

a) The library's central location and hours of operation attract a wide variety of visitors, as intended.

b) Usually anyone may enter, and it is normally not necessary for visitors to answer questions concerning their intentions, or even to speak to anyone else.

c) There is no admission fee, and most services are provided without cost.

d) As a public building full of people, the library may be a good place to look for a victim to those inclined to various forms of criminal activity.

e) There are no metal detectors to pass through or sniffing dogs to pass upon entering.

f) Many library buildings are large structures with secluded areas, private study carrels, and quiet corners.

g) Open stack policies make it possible for people to go more or less where they wish without challenge.

h) Libraries are open for long hours, including after dark, evening hours.

i) Light levels vary in different areas.

j) As public buildings, libraries feature public rest rooms.

k) There are not always staff members or other library personnel working on every floor or in more isolated areas.

l) Low budgets or the desire to make the library an open, inviting place result in few if any security guards or other surveillance personnel.

m) Overworked staff members have so much to deal with in performing their primary duties that they have little time for monitoring public behaviour.

There would seem to be a number of reasons, which singly or in combination may influence the rate of crime:

a) *Direct access to the stacks*: Three hundred thousand of the Library of Congress's 20 million books cannot be accounted for said the Librarian of Congress James Billington in 1992, yet his decision to close the stacks was widely criticised.
b) Placement of high-risk materials such as rare and valuable books either in vulnerable places or in low-visibility areas.
c) Allowing too many staff members access to rare and valuable materials.
d) Having too many keys to the building or to locked cases in circulation among staff.
e) Apathy or indifference about library crime.

Library crime is often not taken seriously by the general public, perhaps because it is seen as unimportant or perhaps because it tends to be seen as victimless crime. The public is too tolerant of misbehaviour and property damage in the public sector. People think it's naughty but not morally wrong, and frequently steal books not out of criminal mentality, but because it costs too much to copy, the photocopier was not working, they did not have change, or the line was too long.

It seems so much easier just to take what you need. An interesting idea would be free photocopying, which could deter the casual or lazy thief, but also might create too much cost for the library. Librarians have had to be concerned with theft since libraries first came into existence, thousands of years ago. Monastic and civil librarians have always attempted to foil crooks.

One thorny aspect of the economics of library security is computing, the price of vandalism and theft. The main problem is that until a book is requested or needed, there is no indication that it is missing. For example, at a large mid-western university, it was recently discovered that almost the entire circulating collection of books on among culture was missing. Although the books were reordered, no one knew exactly how long they had been missing. Circulation statistics contain their check-out dates as well as a wealth of other information.

In several research studies of college students, about half admitted having torn-out pages from library books or magazines at one time or another, while a somewhat smaller yet significant percentage confessed that they had stolen something. A few even admitted that they had done both. If this set of findings is representative of library users in general, then approximately one out of every eight users is a potential thief or vandal.

Inflation also eats away at the budget, but we will leave that factor out of our calculations due to the uncertainty of the rate from year to year. Adding the cost of academic and school library security, and corresponding figures for those special libraries in the public sector, the cost becomes far greater. One library administrator in a large city claims that her library doesn't need a security force because everyone on staff performs security as a part of his or her job description. However, the truth is that libraries probably think it's a lot less expensive to let people take what they like than to make much of an effort to prevent or stop them. Even the staggering financial projections above do nothing to refute the notion that libraries, as public places, present risks to those who enter them, and that library users have a right that they may use such buildings in safety and security.

Most people do not equate libraries with muggers, thieves, perverts, and other dangerous people. Yet libraries are open to the public, and by their very publicness, often serve as magnets for such predators as well as for legitimate patrons. In the language of librarianship, we refer to those who break the rules as 'problem patrons', a blanket term that covers everyone from mild nuisances to extremely violent people.

Library literature provides examples of the endless variety of problem library patrons, including rule breakers of various types, sociopaths, disgruntled spouses, the depressed, the mentally disturbed, the suddenly irate, the paranoid, the eccentric, and even, sometimes, the certifiably insane. Those who work in library buildings expect library patrons to behave in certain ways consistent with their own notions and expectations of proper behaviour.

Today, people expect much more in the way of service and services from libraries than before, and they want it faster or immediately. This attitude can make them aggressive, demanding, and problematical. The rules or procedures may cause problems. They may be impatient or argumentative once they reach the clerk who is taking so long to process materials. They may, on the other hand, be having a particularly bad day, and therefore be unable to prevent their bad mood from leaking into their dealings with other people. Perhaps, part of the problem of irate patrons is the image problem of our profession. Even though we now use computers, we are perceived, even in today's media, as having to do things a certain way, deeply committed to procedures and routines to be followed.

Regardless of objective reality, many members of the public still think that the library is a musty, dusty place, and those who work there are musty, dusty, boring people well suited to those tasks. In most cases, however, expectations of libraries are at odds with our services and capabilities. People want to feel safe and secure wherever they are, whatever they are doing. Most adult patrons want relative quiet and good, efficient service, with their personal safety assumed. If the public feels that the library cannot provide these things together with a safe environment, they will, if they can, go elsewhere to satisfy their information and recreational goals.

Security preparedness from threats involves careful planning and a continual state of vigilance in libraries because they are public buildings. Libraries, mass transit facilities, parks, and museums depend on and even encourage access by the public. Their very existence usually is dependent upon public use and support. Police departments, fire stations, and government agencies, by contrast, are publicly owned, but the public is generally not particularly welcome unless they have business within. Actually, such institutions function more efficiently when access to the public is limited.

As the only public buildings normally open evenings and weekends, libraries attract the homeless and other people who have no place else to go. In a perfect world there would be no need for library security policies, police, or security guards in the library. In our imperfect world, unfortunately, security problems exist in profusion for a variety of reasons.

Of course, one way to cut down severely on security threats in libraries would be for libraries to be places where only those with high-level clearance or permission are permitted access. But erecting barriers to free access would be contrary to most of the reasons that libraries exist in a free society, and the more a library resembles a fortress or a prison, the less free people will feel, once inside. For libraries that do allow public access or even limited access the central question becomes how to maintain open access without being forced to move toward undesirable or undue restrictions on who may enter or what they may do, once inside.

While most library crime is of the small-time chump-change variety, it is crime, nevertheless, and indirectly costs tax-payers money. People are constantly committing crimes in libraries: stealing books, mutilating periodicals, misusing computers, abusing staff verbally, assaulting one another, or otherwise preying upon or harassing other people. Before we can truly discuss crime and other unacceptable behaviours in libraries, however, we must first take a stab at trying to define what is acceptable use of libraries.

However, curiously, just about anybody may enter the public library in most cities with anything they like in their hands, such as briefcases, or notebooks secreted on their persons. This raises a set of security considerations that every library must address, or at least consider seriously if it hopes to safeguard its collections. They include:

a) Building security
b) Equipment security
c) Materials security
d) Personal safety
e) Personal comfort
f) Financial liability
g) Legal issues
h) Problem patrons
i) Ethical issues
j) Electronic security.

People both inside and outside of libraries are stealing or mutilating books and other library materials in significant numbers every day. Precisely how many of our books and other materials disappear is difficult to assess because librarians don't often have a convenient way of noticing such shrinkage, short of a troublesome and time-consuming full-scale inventory, which no one enjoys performing. Perhaps more to the point, librarians do not really like to talk about this vexing and embarrassing problem, which may be one of the reasons why there are no reliable statistics.

In talking about the vast majority of library thieves, we are not referring to hardened criminals, sociopaths, or biblio-kleptomaniacal felons. No, we're talking about those average folks like you and me who are responsible for the sort of minor wrongdoing that will almost never show up on a police report, but that costs the nation's libraries and tax-payers untold millions of dollars in losses every year.

These small-time criminals are everywhere, working their mischief on all types of libraries. Often the motive is not larceny but just plain laziness—it is, after all, easier to tear out the page one wants than it is to copy it, whether the person copies it laboriously by hand or electromechanically by using a coin-operated copy machine. Motive notwithstanding, the result is the same. When a page is removed from a work to satisfy one patron's needs, all other users are deprived of the information on that page.

Whenever personal security is maximised, there is a corresponding diminution of personal liberty. Some people resent this intrusion into their freedom. No one enjoys being searched, interrogated, or denied admission, especially to a tax-supported free library, but some restriction on the use of libraries is inevitable.

Most library crimes are opportunistic in nature and occur when the risk of getting caught is low and the likelihood for success is high. In any case, the typical punishment for getting caught is a nominal fine—the whole situation is usually considered by administration and staff as well as the discovered perpetrator as more embarrassing than serious.

Libraries become easy targets for opportunistic crime because of their policies, their architecture, the lack of vigilance on the part of their employees, and a pervasive view on the part of perpetrators that there is little or no danger of being caught—and even if they are, their punishment will be minimal. The most common criminal activity occurring in libraries is theft or damage to the collections, which are forms of vandalism usually classed as misdemeanours rather than crimes.

Estimates vary, and statistics are notoriously unreliable, but a typical library loses between five and 10 per cent of its collection annually to theft and mutilation, despite all efforts to deter and prevent such crimes. Other crimes of opportunity, including the theft of personal property or library equipment, occur with depressing frequency. Not as common, but still significant, are acts of sexual activity or perversion, especially voyeurism and exhibitionism. Even more frightening is that, in the past few years, verbal and physical abuse of library staff members has been increasing, possibly on the rise because of new addictive drugs that cause their users to become more aggressive while under their influence.

Although most incidents of this nature do not entail actual assault or violence, they are, nevertheless, distressing and disturbing. They are especially problematic since most library staff receive little or no training in how to cope with such abuse, and too many of them work alone or in secluded areas of the building. But the risk of over-confidence is always with us. For one thing, when anyone may walk into a library, there is always the risk of assault. There is always the risk of inside jobs—crimes committed by persons who have been entrusted with the keys or combinations to restricted areas or collections.

The good news is that no security problem is so intractable that it cannot be combated. The bad news is that new security problems crop up all the time. It must also be borne in mind that money is a serious constraint to good security—effective security is always costly, no argument there.

The two-pronged object of all efforts toward library security is that of deterring crime and keeping loss of library property to minimal levels. The best way to deal with crime in a library is to prevent it from happening at all. Another way of putting the same thought is the old saying that an ounce of prevention is worth a pound of cure. Keeping any library collection totally intact may well be an impossible task.

Since we are unlikely to change the behaviour of those who threaten our security, let's at least find and use better means of deterrence, detection, interdiction, apprehension, prosecution, and possibly rehabilitation of those who look upon libraries as prime targets for crime.

Years ago, larger library buildings offered several entrances and exits for the convenience of the public. Now the more safety-conscious libraries have a single public entrance/

exit, and the ones who can afford it post uniformed security guards just inside the doors not only to keep an eye on people entering the building but to make them aware that they are being watched. But the mere presence of guards at the exits isn't sufficient to deter crime. Patrolling the library and checking out all public areas is equally important.

Good security is prohibitively expensive, given typical library budgets. The result is that a number of municipal libraries, and most smaller libraries, cannot afford the simple requirement of at least one security staffer in the building during all hours that the library is open. These libraries, forced to make a choice between good, visible security and more money to spend on materials and public services, usually opt for the latter. The presence of uniformed municipal or campus police, just to remind people that someone trained and equipped to handle problems is on duty for their protection, might be a desirable counter-measure to theft and personal crimes.

Another issue is punishment as a deterrent. However, the punishment for getting caught in various infractions of the law is not terribly severe for most of the crimes against property in libraries. In cases of crimes against people, law enforcement usually takes a stricter approach to punishment.

In the case of crimes against property, however—such as the theft of a single book or two—few libraries are willing to go to the trouble of pressing charges, and most library administrations profess themselves to be happy just to have their books returned. But in the United States, where personal freedoms are prized above just about anything else, there are limits to punishment that most people would deem appropriate.

While safekeeping of a library's collection is of great importance, personal safety is far more important, because human lives may be at stake. Books, videos, and even computers can be repaired or replaced, but such is not the case with people. The primary objective of all security precautions in libraries is to discourage crime and misdemeanours, whether the infraction in question concerns the illegal removal of books from the collection, the filching of wallets from unattended purses, or a range of violent acts.

Most library buildings are, by their nature, places where all are free to enter, which unfortunately puts everyone at risk. And some buildings, due to surrounding neighbourhood, design faults, layout, or lighting, are more conducive to violent incidents than others. Too many nooks and crannies in the stacks mean security personnel and other staff must patrol these places frequently.

Some library staff work in isolated sections of a large building, which presents an additional problem for security. While these circumstances cannot always be avoided, paying extra attention to these areas through monitors or security phones is one approach. And there is no excuse for poor lighting in any remote area of the library.

Besides sharp-eyed staff and security personnel, however, there are a variety of weapons available in the library's arsenal against crime. Some of them are:

a) Closed-circuit television cameras
b) Electronically accessed entryways
c) Alarms on exit doors
d) Access authorization cards
e) Sign-in sheets
f) Placing facilities and equipment in high-visibility areas.

A few public libraries now require patrons to show a library card to gain admittance. This seemingly harsh measure followed repeated incidents in which pages had been ripped from magazines and reference books, materials stolen, rest rooms misused, and staff members verbally abused. The thinking is that if all visitors know that they are identified and known to staff, fewer of them will be rash or foolish enough to risk being caught committing a crime or misdemeanour. When it comes to personal safety, however, people sit up and take notice, especially in the wake of some crime involving the personal injury of a library patron or staff member. This book's main task is to publicise some problems of protecting libraries, and to present practical ideas and effective security methods. Library employees, and their security staffs, are the first line of defence. The issues connected to library security—collection and equipment preservation and personal and public security—are intertwined.

Library security is still evolving, and those charged with preserving both materials and public safety are always experimenting with new things to see what works. There is one obvious solution to library crime, but one that many libraries are disinclined to use—prosecute those caught committing misdeeds. Get tough and get serious about security. Commitment to the goal of getting tough with those who commit offences against library materials or property would help a lot.

Mutilating library materials is a crime under state and municipal statutes in almost all communities, although librarians are characteristically disinclined to follow through and press charges. Sometimes, however, lack of time to follow through is as serious a disincentive to getting serious with criminals as is lack of will.

Today, global libraries use network security policies to ensure the implementation of their security model, in maintaining network security, protection of information loss, alteration, unavailability, and the safeguarding of the organisation's network form internal and external threats. These implementations have often been neglected by users within an organisation, due to their misinterpretations, mis-understandings, lack in responsibilities and involvement towards information security in the organisation. For this reason a security awareness policy was developed to ensure that all users involve in a computerised environment, to be on the lookout for any security risks that might occur. This awareness reduces the likelihood for threats from happening, and involves the user to take corrective steps if risks are being identified.

Some ways for every user to approach information security, and how to sharpen their awareness towards security concerns, by contributing to these issues are given below:

a) Apply all password recommendations and features.

b) Report any suspicious activity immediately.

c) Never leave your workstation unattended.

e) Take note of any security documentation received.

f) Scan data and files regularly for viruses.

g) Always attend all security meetings and courses.

h) Never share user privileges.

i) Do not exceed user rights.

j) Alert your superior if your security identity has been revealed.

k) Never repair security problems yourself.

l) Apply all password recommendations and features.

For any computer system, an appropriate password is of high importance. Passwords should be kept secret at all time, never shared with anyone, or stored on the workstation unless encrypted. Suspicious system activities, files missing from the system, and unrecognised user IDs should immediately be reported to any superior or system administrator.

All users should protect their workstation when leaving for lunch or a small break. Workstations are most vulnerable when left unattended and should be protected. Methods to protect workstations may include the use of a special hot button to enable the protective mode when out, or the use of a screen saver password. All files and data kept on the workstation should regularly be scanned for viruses. Viruses come out all the time and all systems should have the latest virus updates installed. No data downloaded from outside connections, like the internet or received form unknown sources should be trusted and immediately checked for viruses. Meetings regarding security issues is vital to alert the user about important matters and always should be attended to.

Courses should be integrated to extend the users' knowledge about awareness and all new staff is obliged to attend the recommended security course. User identities should never be shared with anyone, regardless the fact that he/she might be the users best friend, family member, staff member, etc. Only the user himself may use his identity and privileges. Tokens, access cards, pin numbers or whatever security mechanism may not be shared between anyone and should immediately be reported if lost or stolen.

Unauthorised system log-ons may mislead system personnel and distract them from real threats. Users should always arrange with their system administrator if they are in need of information, or require access to essential resources that is out of reach. The security manager or other security personnel should immediately be alerted whenever the users' security identity or key have been revealed. This might happen when the user accidentally revealed their password, or access card being lost or stolen. Whenever there is a system failure, unauthorised access or data exploitation, users should restore changes by notifying the system personnel, instead of repairing the problem themselves.

Users should share problems and recommendations among their colleagues. Shared experiences help users and management improve the awareness approach, and highlight the importance of these implementations in safeguarding the organisation. Management should play a very distinctive role in the establishment of a well-defined awareness policy, by means of an organisational strategy approach. Users should follow the awareness aspects and implement their skills to strengthen the system.

The organisational structure divides the awareness strategy from top management to lower levels to ensure changes are globally recognised. Top management should acknowledge the need for the awareness approach, by means of the security concerns, and give responsibility among senior management with a follow-up request at a given point of time. Senior management should organise the responsibility in a more comparative way, and take corrective action if security measures have not been implemented. Their tasks consist in the development of an awareness policy and implementation strategy among users.

Security manager should be in charge of controlling and organising the implementation strategy developed by the senior management. All the awareness plans and policies should be reviewed, with given input if needed. System administrators should be responsible for the operation and proper functioning of the system. They have to ensure that users comply with the security regulations, assist users with their responsibilities and monitor awareness strategies for maximum efficiency. Users should strictly follow the recommendations and policies provided to them, and follow the regulations to ensure reliability and effectiveness. All new personnel have to take part in the awareness course, this is essential to establish a healthy understanding of security concerns. New staff will be inducted into the awareness strategy in the following way:

a) Receives an information resources security manual.
b) Understands his/her responsibilities as a user of information resources.
c) Can identify information security resources.
d) Understands the security awareness policies.
e) Can identify examples of sensitive and/or confidential data in his/her department.
f) Understands the repercussions of security violations.
g) Discuss groups and previous problems.

To keep uptodate with security matters and findings, discussion groups and meetings should occur on a regular basis, to allow users to share their problems and solutions they discovered. These activities are important to enlighten concerns the organisation may experience, and how to handle these in a proper way. Monthly meetings are to be held in the discussions of security-related issues. The purpose of these meetings is strictly to encourage users to improve their awareness skills.

Success of various awareness implementations like messages, training courses, external testing and how it affects the system should be included in the discussion, with ways to be more effective in assessing risks and to add improvements to. Methods involving awareness of inside difficulties and system usage. External groups investigate strengths and weaknesses. The system should always be kept free from internal errors. Users may oversee their own faults and possible threats that might endanger the system. To ensure that most security problems have been addressed, and to avoid a subjective approach to the system, it is important to use an external specialist. External specialists and consultants should do a thorough investigation on the environment and identify systems failures with recommendations. These findings are important for internal users in the identification of vulnerabilities, to sharpen their security awareness.

Implementation of a new system may result in great effectiveness for the organisation, or might have disastrous consequences. Users might not be aware of the functionality and usage of the system, and this may influence the effectiveness of security. Users should be clearly informed about the functions of the system, by undergoing training courses to improve their adaptability to the changes, and to ensure they understand all security implementations of the system. Users should always be aware of important matters and decisions within the organisation, to be more alert users about serious security issues.

Important security topics in emails or weekly newsletters should regularly be reviewed for relevant information as the following:

a) Virus warnings about active viruses on the system, or via e-mail.
b) Unsafe internet sites that should be avoided.
c) Flaws in current software versions that should be upgraded.
d) Software that should not be downloaded.
e) Attacks that happened on the system.
f) Visual awareness methods.

Methods to be activated in improving awareness include the following:

a) *Use of a key holder*: Key holders with a random generated digital password. The key holder is synchronised with the company's passwords server and every password is unique. The user should always be in possession of the key holder and supply the password when needed to access the system.
b) *Flyers, stationery and gifts*: Use of flyers and banners results as a good strategy to improve awareness among users. Invitations such as a security awareness week and security seminars could be distributed via this technique. Stationary and gift with security phrases may be used to create a more positive attitude towards user involvement and awareness.
c) *Workstation reminders*: Workstation reminders are helpful when passwords need to be changed or for new implementations by the user. A workstation reminder like screen warnings, or dialogue boxes could be implemented to alert users about these changes.
d) *Reminders via network messages*: Network messages via pop-up dialogues are an efficient way of reminding users

about their security responsibilities. These kinds of messages may reach a vast number of users instantly. The security that responsibilities send should contain matters that may seek immediate attention and be used for warnings like system shutdown, network virus invasion, network drives not to be accessed or files not to be downloaded or installed

e) *Internet awareness*: A special focus about internet usage should be implemented. All users should be educated about the dangers of internet applications, and be familiarised of what content might be malicious, with the necessary browser security settings in place. Internet restrictions should be specified implicitly, in stipulating what user rights and privileges are acceptable. This strategy furthermore involve ways of notifying users to download and send information in the right manner, and how to avoid misuse of internet privileges may leave the system vulnerable to outside attacks.

To maximise an organisation's investment in security, indeed for that investment to make any sense at all, it is vital that the level of awareness of security issues among all employees of the organisation be maximised. The result of a successful security policy lies in efficiency of user commitment towards organisational security, their close interaction in ensuring secure system functionality, and the implementation of a successful security strategy with management plan.

While information security programmes are sometimes implemented following an actual loss or incident, prudent business organisations address security early in their corporate life. For most business enterprises, the concern for physical security is best understood and, as a result, addressed first. However, information security puts the emphasis on protecting the information stored in or processed by the system rather than focusing on simply protecting equipment.

In the modern business environment, profitability and survivability depend on information. Regardless of the enterprise's business, all of the corporate data resident on the enterprise's computer systems is both valuable and vulnerable. Since today's business enterprise has extensive electronic communication pathways extending well beyond the physical bounds of the business operation, internal vulnerabilities may be exploited by external threats as well as internal. The consequences can be loss or modification of critical business data, disruption of services, compromise of proprietary business plans or processes. Even well-protected businesses may be vulnerable to attacks on corporate web pages. There are trivial attacks that will give access to the source of a corporate web page to any intruder.

Today, there often exists a conflict between security objectives and operational requirements. Marketing, finance, engineering, and management all produce and use data that are critical to that organisation's business activities. In addition, within the government or the defence industry, some of this data could be considered classified or unclassified but sensitive, requiring even stricter controls for its protection.

Despite the pressure to overlook security needs, successful and responsible organisations will have a written security policy and formal security plans and procedures in place to guide their employees, as well as their business, in protecting their computing assets. Management is able to quantify the benefits of a security programme as a function of costs.

To formalise this analysis process, certain concepts must be considered. These include:

a) A business risk is anything that could potentially harm the operation, assets, or profitability of the organisation.
b) Risk analysis is a formal process of determining what your computing assets are worth, identifying vulnerabilities by discovering where threats/exposures could occur, and then determining how much potential harm could be caused if the identified vulnerabilities were exploited.

c) For each vulnerability identified, the risk analysis produces a cost-benefit analysis to determine if the cost to implement fixes or increase protection is justified by the cost of the asset's loss.

Security policies and risk go hand in hand. A policy is needed to reduce risk, and the risk analysis is used to justify a security policy.

If management and employees understand their respective responsibilities for protecting computer data, it follows that they must also recognise the problems they face in developing and implementing a security programme. Management has the ultimate responsibility for implementing a data security programme based on an assessment of business risk and an information system (IS) security risk assessment. All levels of management must be involved to insure the programme is understood and properly implemented.

The management must understand that they are legally responsible for the integrity of corporate data assets just as they are with other assets of the corporation. Employees must recognise that the corporate data on their computers is both valuable and vulnerable. They must understand their legal responsibilities regarding the unauthorised release of sensitive data. Sensitive data means data that requires protection due to the risk and magnitude of loss or harm that could result from its unavailability, disclosure, alteration, or destruction.

User awareness training is one of the most common means available to achieve recognition of responsibility and computing asset worth. Some organisations require personnel to sign an agreement that includes the protection of computing assets as a condition of employment, while others sign agreements as a condition of allowing their connection to the organisations network. The related responsibilities for various management levels within a typical corporation are given below:

a) *Chairman of the board*: To protect and insure for continuity of the corporation.

b) *President*: To protect and insure for profitability of the corporation.

c) *Managers*: To maintain information as a strategic asset of the corporation.

d) *IS security manager*: To insure written security policies are developed, implemented and followed.

e) *Users*: Ultimate responsibility for accidental or intentional destruction or disclosure.

Operational IS security is not a direct concern of upper management, but the protection of information assets certainly is. The IS security manager is the key to development and enforcement of a comprehensive security policy. Without this individual physically inserted into the management process, a security programme will not be implemented or enforceable, and upper management will not be able to provide for the protection of its information assets.

IS vulnerabilities in general, relate to the weak points of the tangible computing assets in the corporation, and how exposed these assets might be to exploitation. These vulnerabilities can vary greatly depending on the network or stand-alone environment used by the corporation. Obviously, the weakest link in the security chain is also the most vulnerable point. Since the three basic goals of computer security are ensuring secrecy, integrity, and availability of data, vulnerabilities of a computer-oriented business can include just about everything related to the business operation.

Employee motivation is a key feature of computer security. The disgruntled employee who imports or develops a virus generally does so for revenge. He wishes to get back at management for that tiny raise, or the overlooked promotion. Crackers who break into protected networks or sensitive files are motivated by peer pressure or simply entertainment. Industrial spies could be driven by political or financial reasons. Regardless of motivation, the personal perspective of individuals who have access to corporate computing assets is of critical importance. Individuals who have access to corporate computing assets are those who have the opportunity to create problems. This opportunity not only relates to employees, but also to those who are external to the corporation but might gain access based on weak network protection techniques.

2
Library Security Methods

The role of all security precautions and actions is to manage and minimise the risk of security problems occurring. The types of security with regard to libraries as public buildings are: security of occupants of the building, a master plan consisting of operating procedures for staff, security personnel, and the public to follow. Sources of risk to libraries are theft or damage to its collection, violent behaviour perpetrated against others in the building, and physical damage to the building or facilities by vandalism, accident, or one of a number of other events. As a library staff member, you have an obligation to all who enter the building to provide a safe environment for them to use the facilities.

Planning of library security is a sequential process involving several factors, which should follow a logical progression. Asset definition is a good way to begin the process. Ask yourself what is to be protected and what level of security is needed for each type of asset. Such assets include property, information, and people. Once assets to be protected have been defined or at least described, we then move on to defining some of the potential threats to each asset and who would be likely to act them out. It is equally important to calculate how likely such threats are to happen.

A library security team is to be formed headed by the member of the staff designated as Library Security Officer (LSO), who should meet periodically to discuss and deal with such matters as security responsibility. Designation of a

Library Security Officer from among existing staff and writing a situation-specific building security manual are paramount. Preparation also involves the team's anticipation and discussion of security and safety problems. Knowing the appropriate laws and rules and what security officers are permitted or supposed to do is equally important and may require consultation with legal officers or representatives. A security team is highly recommended for every library of every size and type. The team should either personally conduct or delegate someone to conduct a security audit of the entire building. Several access issues will surface during this security audit stage.

Since total security is an unobtainable goal, the object of a periodic security audit should not be an attempt to make the library absolutely safe. The security team should consider and analyse various types and levels of security measures possible, with projected costs. The building audit should pay special attention to such matters as entrances and exits, other means of access, and security screening devices.

In conducting the audit, the team should ask itself what, if any, are the design or redesign implications of bolstering security in the library, how much remodelling will be necessary to upgrade the library's security posture, and what it will cost. Other variables that the library may or will be forced to deal with include such issues as ongoing maintenance contracts, metal detectors at doorways, armed versus unarmed security forces, staff training for security operations, surveillance cameras inside and outside the building, glass breakage detectors, video surveillance, door and other intrusion alarms, delay devices, thermal sensors and alarms, duress alarms, scream alarms, and fire alarms.

SECURITY PLAN

The library's security plan document should be designed to make criminal behaviour so difficult that it occurs infrequently or not at all. Here are some steps to preparing a security and public safety plan:

a) Analyse the potential for unauthorised access to non-public areas.

b) Discuss with staff various responses to armed or dangerous intruders.

c) Install or upgrade access controls and surveillance equipment.

d) Regularly review the effectiveness and roles of security personnel.

e) Distribute an uptodate security and safety checklist to all staff.

f) Work on improving and clarifying communications lines among staff and with police, fire department, and so on.

g) At least once a year, involve all employees in a full-scale simulated practical exercise to rehearse their roles in an incident involving a threat to public safety.

h) Orient new employees to emergency procedures.

i) Train new employees in emergency procedures as part of their orientation.

While public safety is everyone's job in the library, there is frequently lack of consensus or disagreement among administration and library staff on several points.

a) Lack of agreement about the balance between access and protection.

b) Different views on funding priorities.

c) Lack of commitment on the part of city, academic institution, or library administrators to enforcement of safety procedures.

d) Lack of coordination among library staff, security force, and police.

e) Lack of awareness in the criminal justice system to the problem and magnitude of library crime.

f) Lack of resolve or knowing what to do on the part of staff members in dealing with non-incidents in the library.

There is just no telling who is going to walk through the front door next. It is natural that people are going to exhibit a wide range of problem behaviours, each requiring a different approach, none guaranteed or foolproof. What works with one difficult individual on a given day may not work on other individuals on the same day, nor will it necessarily prove effective with the same individual on a different day.

For proof of this assertion, let us say for the sake of convenience that there are four alternative solutions to a problem behaviour in the library:

a) Ignore the behaviour and encourage others to do the same.

b) Gently talk to the offensive party and try to persuade him or her to stop.

c) Firmly request or demand that the offender stop or you will call security or the police immediately.

d) Call security or the police immediately.

With regard to libraries as public buildings, there are various important security considerations. The master plan, consisting of standard or recommended operating procedures for staff, security personnel, and the public should address each of these problems to the extent that they can be anticipated. Security personnel, where present, should be consulted and included in planning procedures.

The sources of risk to libraries are theft or damage to its collection, violent behaviour perpetrated against others in the building, and physical damage to the building or facilities by vandalism, accident, or any of a number of other events. Every library staff member has an obligation to all who enter the building to provide a safe environment in which they may use facilities with a minimum of risk. Good security, however, is going to be expensive, and very good security is going to be very expensive. Some workable compromise between tight security and no security at all is possible and must be found so that the public is comfortable with any inconvenience and materials and people are reasonably protected from harm, intrusion, or loss.

Security personnel and various anti-theft devices are highly recommended, but while each of them has its costs, each offers its own rewards. Deliberate and thoughtful planning for emergency situations in the library is very important and should be accomplished to the extent possible before such situations occur. According to the Smithsonian Institution's *Guidelines for Library and Archives Security*, every library, as an institution open to the public yet entrusted with the protection of valuable property, should enact policies and procedures with regard to matters such as:

a) fire protection
b) emergency protection
c) physical barrier and lock and key protection
d) security staff protection
e) personal access and property control protection
f) security alarms and electronics protection.

Security procedures should be carefully thought out and discussed with all library staff, involving such concerns as minimising risk; rapid, firm, and consistent response; remaining calm; drill evacuation procedures; a telephone tree to alert other departments; the role of security guards; and role-playing games and simulated emergencies to elicit and evaluate possible responses to threats.

Management must endorse and support both the goals and the strategies of interdiction and discouragement of potential perpetrators. Most of the following actions can be taken immediately by most libraries and have the additional advantage of not requiring much in the way of new funding:

a) Safety seminars, workshops and in-service training sessions should be scheduled on a regular basis to train all staff for dealing with confrontation and recognising and knowing how to cope with threats, attitudes, and warning signs.

b) A crisis management plan should be in place and reviewed with all staff members.

c) Liaison with local law enforcement agencies should be maintained or upgraded, where possible.

d) All rules pertinent to library security should be posted in conspicuous places.

e) The library should affirm its willingness to prosecute in cases of crime committed against people or property.

f) Monitoring of rest rooms should be a daily part of staff duties.

g) Well-marked emergency phones or communications devices should be placed outside the libraries.

Security is everybody's business because it affects everybody's safety. However, we might wish it otherwise, library crime exists and is going to continue to exist as long as there are libraries. It therefore behaves us to do what we can to prevent crime as a preferable and cheaper alternative to dealing with crimes outbreak or its aftermath and repercussions. The combined attempts of library staff and others can go a long way toward mitigating the potential for breaches of normal safety and security. Such mitigation activities are designed to reduce the degree of long-term risk to human life and property from natural and manufactured hazards alike.

The simplest way to reduce security problems is to make the most likely trouble spots less attractive to thieves, sexual deviants, and others bent on crime or mischief. Specific remedies may be to add lighting that cannot be altered; to move or create an employee work area or staging area for shelving in or near these areas; to arrange some sort of activity in the area that is also productive for the library, like shelf reading, bar-coding, or shifting shelves to make room for new books.

Perhaps, persons caught violating laws should be prosecuted, regardless of who is caught, and their prosecution should be publicised. It must be made known that this behaviour is not condoned by the library administration, will not be tolerated, and those caught will be prosecuted vigorously. Further, the public should be aware that library theft or mutilation has real-world consequences severe enough to deter would-be criminals or opportunists from contemplating adding the library to the short list of their favourite haunts and hang-outs. A proactive library is one that has prepared itself for quick reaction to security problems. However, legal statutes or existing guidelines can impede efforts for that reaction to be instituted. It is important to know where the library stands—both legally and practically—regarding problem behaviour by members of the public.

Libraries open to the public exist to serve the public but usually can define their public and the services to be rendered as they see them. For instance, some services, such as borrowing privileges, may apply only to those who can prove residency within the taxing district. Some libraries allow a nominal initial borrowing of only a few items, as a safeguard against untrustworthiness, in case they never see their materials again. The actual library card is mailed to the patron at the address stated on the application.

Some libraries issue membership cards only if the card-seeker brings in a recent utility bill or other official correspondence with his or her name on it. This is only good sense and protection of the public interest. When library materials are purchased with tax dollars, the whole community has a financial stake in their cost. Librarians lend, but do not give, materials to patrons. They expect these materials to be returned in a timely fashion or renewed. Like all other custodians and guardians, librarians must be accountable to their funding source for the proper management of the items in their charge.

Sometimes missing articles can be recovered, but recovery of overdue and lost items can become problematical in a number of ways, and it is normally safer and saner to make a serious attempt to hold on to things before they walk out of the door than it is to try to get them back afterward. This is yet another proof of the adage about the ounce of prevention, and it is good business sense as well. Like any other business, the library must know how to get in touch with its customers.

To qualify for availing oneself of library services, a valid identification card with address and photo may be necessary. Non-members of the library's community may be extended privileges, but fairness requires that they incur charges commensurate with the taxes paid by residents of the jurisdiction for their borrowing privileges. Sometimes patrons refuse to provide personal information. When such patrons are notified that we view them as risky borrowers, they become problem patrons if they begin arguing with the desk staff over procedures and policies.

Many unpleasant incidents, however, can be averted or avoided if we have spelled out ahead of time just who is entitled to what, and do not deviate from established policy no matter who is concerned. It is also unwise to keep the rules hidden or to make them up as you go along to suit the situation. Sometimes patrons actually ask to see the rules in writing or ask how long and why a particular rule has been in effect. We should have positive and prompt answers to these questions ready for them. The rules must apply uniformly and evenly to all who enter the library or we are going to have problems and possibly be charged with discrimination.

Patrons come from a variety of backgrounds, experiences, and levels of literacy. However we do it, we must find ways to communicate the rules. All patrons need to know about them, and we cannot assume that the public knows anything about us or what we do. This is why it is important to review, distribute, and reiterate the rules of our library to all. We must require them to bring appropriate identification, if we use it to determine the borrowing eligibility. We must let them know ahead of time the penalties that they will incur should they fail to return materials on time. It is also important to post rules and board-sanctioned policies concerning proper conduct within the library's walls.

We must be both vigilant and diligent about educating both our public and our staff. This proactive approach will, in the long run, serve to cut down on complaints and misunderstandings and to improve public relations. The cornerstone to solving the problem patron issue is a strong and supportive administration. There are too many problem patron scenarios in library literature in which nothing useful could be done by the staff to address the problem because they had no authority or support from the administration.

Libraries may find themselves behind the curve in keeping up. Being proactive means that we cannot wait until a problem occurs and then develop a policy. If it was written five, ten, or even more years ago, chances are that things would have changed to the extent that changes are needed in the policies. Perhaps teen gangs did not harass patrons at the library some years ago but have begun to do so now. Some parents have always used the library as a baby-sitting or day-care service, but in times of economic uncertainty, their numbers grow. Panhandling, theft of personal property, sexual harassment, and indecent display may not have occurred to the policy/guideline writers of a generation ago as problems, but they are often more problematic today.

The language of your library's behaviour policy will reflect not just your conditions, objectives, and goals, but something in the rules ought to state that any person in the library whose behaviour falls outside the guidelines may be asked to leave by library personnel, be evicted from the premises by security officers, or be subject to arrest by police. In public libraries, this language should be consistent with relevant provisions of local municipal civil and criminal codes.

Academic institutions may have a code of student conduct that governs behaviour on campus, which will normally apply to library users as well. These are good sources to start with because they should delineate prohibitions and rights. Academic campuses, in addition to having their own rules, are not exempt from state or federal laws that cover all other citizens. If necessary, library security officers may need to discuss these issues with the local police to find out which behaviours are not allowed in public what laws exist, apply, and are enforceable; and what recourse is available.

Every library worker at a public workstation will hear many times during a long career some aggrieved member of the public protesting. A library that maintains a good rapport with local police and social service agencies is more likely to get a quick response to its requests for assistance than one that has never bothered.

SECURITY STAFFS

Every library should appoint someone from the existing staff as Library Security Officer (LSO), and that officer should be charged with coordination of staff efforts should include compilation of inventories. This may simply be noting the loss of a few items, or it may mean an extensive inventory of the entire collection, which may take months. The FBI may not be willing to enter a case unless the value of the missing material can be judged sufficiently substantial that felony charges can be anticipated in the event an arrest is made. Prompt and candid communication to staff about progress on the case is also a good idea. Creation and maintenance of internal records of actions followed during the progress of the case must be undertaken. Names, telephone numbers, and addresses should be included when appropriate.

Information can be used to assure trustees and insurers that appropriate actions have been taken or are in the works. And each new law enforcement officer or detective assigned to the case can be brought up to speed quickly by reading such journal entries. Library theft is serious business. It needs legal prosecution like other transgressions and infractions. One can only hope that librarians will take their concerns to their state or provincial legislatures and demand improvement where inadequate state laws exist.

A library's staffing may leave its security at risk, too. During evening and weekend hours, student assistants may be the mainstay of library services. Week-nights, full-time library employees may work only at the reference and government documents, desks until 9 pm. Circulation staff members may rotate evening and weekend duties, and might be the only full-time staff available in an emergency situation.

Security guards are responsible for securing the library at closing and are trusted with access to keys normally unavailable to other library workers. These duties require the maturity to assume responsibility and authority and to make quick, accurate judgements in an emergency or problem situation. Guards may have served in the military or even be retired from the police force.

Most academic libraries share certain characteristics that make them especially vulnerable. The very nature of the function of libraries, in fact, lends itself to criminal activity in that the library expects its assets to be taken off the premises free of charge and brought back at a later date. Even more problematically, academic libraries tend to be open beyond normal business hours and are accessible more hours than other buildings on campus. Most have large open stack areas and are sparsely staffed after the end of the business day and on weekends.

Study carrels may dot the stack areas, and these are ideal places for various forms of crime. The fact that libraries are usually rather pleasant places, with normally friendly staff, makes academic libraries, especially those in or near urban areas, attractive to the homeless and mentally ill. First among alternate security options would be the employment of uniformed police to patrol and maintain a presence in the building during all hours of operation.

Even one uniformed professional security guard provides a psychological level of security and a deterrent to opportunists as well. But private security may have problems, too, including high turnover, inadequate training, inconsistent supervision, sleeping or reading on duty, and being out of sight for long periods of time. One library reported thefts by the security guards. University libraries often are empowered to station security employees in their buildings.

They are normally paid at substantially lower wages than career security guards but are taught skills to deal effectively with unruly or belligerent persons and to look for suspicious circumstances and persons. Their duties include random interior patrols, external checks of the building, and a preclosing security check. Such patrols, provided that selection is careful, can be a successful deterrent to theft, mutilation, and rule violation. Student security monitors are often contracted through campus police departments that may hire, schedule, train them in basic security procedures, provide uniforms, and supervise them.

The library and the campus police should jointly develop a detailed job description for use in training the monitors in specific library procedures. Such monitors provide a presence by being easily recognisable as security personnel. By regularly being seen throughout the buildings, they act as deterrents to potential violations of library policy and/or the law. They can also investigate deviant and potentially threatening behaviour and coordinate obtaining police assistance, if needed. They may be used at closing to check the outside exits to make sure they are locked and properly secured. Additionally, at closing, monitors clear unstaffed areas of the library and assist public service staff in clearing and securing their areas.

Student monitors can be expected to check the integrity of the alarms on all emergency exits on a monthly basis, and to assist in the evacuation of the buildings during emergency situations. A persistent problem stems from the lack of library control over the monitors, who work for the campus police. Some monitors don't appear to receive adequate training. All too often, two monitors may decide to patrol together. They share a conversation, their attention not on their duties, even though one is supposed to patrol the building while the other remains at the desk. When times are slow, monitors study, sleep, or sit for long periods of time, reading while on duty instead of patrolling.

Many academic libraries have taken repeated measures over the years to remedy such situations but the problems persist. By way of solution to such problems, a very specific checklist of duties should be compiled by library staff and sent to campus police, along with the library's evacuation plan, copies of which should be distributed to all security monitors. An hourly head count may be required so that the monitors have to walk through the library to all the public service points at least once an hour to count patrons and have public service staff initial their headcount sheet. The ideal situation would be to hire security guards as members of the library staff to be on duty during all hours that the library is open.

Advantages of this plan for the library include the opportunity to make hiring and firing decisions; the ability to employ library performance standards, including merit raises or other rewards for good performance, as well as immediate reprimands; and control of training. Employee loyalty because of long-term employment is also a benefit. Since they are library staff, uniformed officers may also be trained to help out at circulation and in the stacks when necessary, where their contracts do not prohibit such practices.

Unlike their academic counterparts, public libraries, do not normally have the luxury of prohibiting people from using their facility, and their guards must be extremely circumspect in what they are allowed to do in dealing with suspicious patrons. As a *de facto*, if not *de jure*, public building, the public library is open to all who walk through the doors. Most people who use a public library employ it for library purposes reading for recreation or information, studying, and so on.

It is the minority of people who do not use the library for library purposes who cause headaches for the library's staff. Many public libraries, as previously mentioned, simply do not have security staff, for the simple reason that the hiring of such employees is beyond their budgets. The public library's security staff should, where funds permit, carry walkie-talkies while they are on duty. This permits them to converse with each other and makes them easy to reach and to summon police quickly if they need help.

The primary responsibility of library security staff is to check bags, backpacks, and similar items to prevent theft. Such responsibility is especially important on schooldays. During the hours between the time when the school is dismissed and closing time, monitors should patrol the library. They are instructed to be alert for noisy or disruptive people, vandalism attempts, harassing or stalking behaviour, and other possible threats against library property or users.

Periodic meetings help maintain lines of communication. Having uniformed police visible from time to time on the library's grounds deters many potential troublemakers from coming into the library, while having police patrol the building on no fixed schedule will go a long way to deterring crime. Drug dealing is the most common infraction, and when the practice is observed, staff should call police immediately and not attempt to deal with such behaviours themselves.

Although gang members and wanna-bees may loiter on the public library grounds, they usually do not bring their battles into the facility, for which we should all be grateful. Fortunately, libraries are not normally declared a specific gang's turf, although showing of colours goes on all the time in urban libraries, and that could lead to incidents within the library's walls. While there may be fights outside library buildings, however, including some that spill over from nearby schools, there are relatively few such problems inside the building.

Library security staff are not empowered to intervene in criminal behaviour that they may witness outside the building's walls, but should quickly contact the police when such behaviour is observed. Besides the difficulties described, the most common problem is vandalism. It appears in two forms: vandalism to the library building, furniture, or equipment, and mutilation of library materials. Tagging is the current slang term for the practice of individuals or gang members intentionally marking a wall or other surface to declare their existence or affiliation.

Library buildings have many blank walls and other surfaces that attract vandals. Security and custodial staff should be instructed to watch for graffiti, and work as promptly as they can to clean taggers' markings from the building and elevators. Unfortunately, security staff, short of catching perpetrators in the act, have no way of monitoring these activities, although placing a hidden video camera in public areas or the elevators may help to catch vandals. More frustrating to librarians and users alike is the constant mutilation of materials, not a problem unique to public libraries, but epidemic within them.

Librarians discover missing items almost daily. Within a short period of time, recently at one California urban public library, staff members noted that maps had been torn from encyclopedias, large reference books, textbooks, atlases, and biographical sources. Complicating matters, such books are often out of print and cannot be replaced. Despite security systems in place, missing items still form a large part of the typical public library's security problem. These fall into three categories: materials that are actually stolen, materials hidden or mis-shelved deliberately, and items checked out and not returned.

Security staff are normally vigilant when they are at their stations at the library exit, but they cannot always catch everyone leaving the library and ask to inspect their bags. Obviously, unless or until libraries can security-tag every page of every item, they will never apprehend all those who vandalise materials. Some libraries have gone to the extreme of employing collection agencies to retrieve materials by calling—or even visiting—delinquent borrowers and demanding that they return the overdue materials. But such moves may backfire: The compensation of the collectors frequently outweighs the value of the missing items, and even if they force a delinquent borrower to pay the cost of the lost items, such items are frequently out of print or otherwise unavailable.

There are no inexpensive or easy solutions to these chronic public library problems. Certainly, an expanded and visible security force can act as a deterrent. Private security guards on duty during the afternoon and evening help a great deal, and staff should be vigilant against vandalism, whether by taggers or mutilators of library materials. Many public libraries have attempted to interdict loss of their materials by purchasing and installing checkpoint or other stop-loss devices to provide material security. Such systems operate on the principle that magnetised materials will trigger an alarm and lock a turnstile, thus preventing the thief from making off with purloined books.

Public libraries do not have a campus rules book or academic code to fall back on. However, local statutes that apply to all public places may serve as working guidelines. If necessary, library staff should discuss these issues with the local police to find out what behaviours are not allowed in public; what laws exist, apply, and are enforceable; and what recourse we have. This takes time, but it will save aggravation later.

LIBRARY SECURITY GUIDELINES

The *Library Security Guidelines* is a document based on work done in 1996 under the auspices of the Smithsonian Institution by an intern from Buena Vista University in Storm Lake, Iowa. The project was managed by David Liston, the Smithsonian's Protection Outreach Officer, who has developed a similar document for museums. The document has been revised by a subcommittee of the Safety and Security Committee, Buildings and Equipment Section, Library Administration and Management Association (LAMA), a division of the American Library Association. Guidelines are not standards, and this document does not attempt to establish standards. While some industry standards are recommended, the use of the term standard in no way implies that libraries that do not adopt the recommendations are in any way negligent.

Libraries are so diverse that there will be those for which these guidelines do not apply. While the recommendations are voluntary, they represent the composite opinion of the leading experts in the field of library security as being appropriate for most, if not all, libraries. Smaller libraries will not have the staff necessary to comply with some guidelines. Many libraries do not have a director of security or even a security force and should not be obligated to hire a staff member specifically to serve as director of security.

In adopting the spirit of the guidelines, the small library will designate one person to hold this title and be responsible for these duties in addition to his or her regular duties. Successful library security programmes are based on clearly defined and well-communicated behaviour policies for public and for staff. Although these guidelines do not explicitly refer to rules of conduct for the public or staff, the guidelines are based on the assumption that the library has a set of rules governing public and staff conduct in place. Behaviour policies or rules of conduct are a local responsibility that will be unique to each library setting, but these policies should be reviewed by the library's legal counsel and approved officially by the library's governing body. Security personnel will have a very difficult time enforcing behaviour rules if these rules are not clearly communicated to the public and staff. Even in the library with its own security force, the security officers can only be in one place at a time. It is everyone's responsibility to ensure that both public and staff have a safe environment.

Duty to Protect

The library director, or designee in safety and security matters, should be responsible for:

i) Safeguarding the physical protection of both library employees and library patrons. He/she also is responsible for protecting the building, its contents, and its immediate surroundings. This responsibility includes, but is not limited to, the development and integration of protection programmes for fires, floods, earthquakes, and other natural disasters.

ii) Ensuring that library employees are informed and instructed of their obligations in safety and security matters, for example, the obligation to protect lives and collections, to provide aid to disaster victims, etc.

iii) Taking all reasonable steps to minimise loss and damage to collections, furniture, and equipment.

iv) Developing and integrating a library asset protection policy that addresses, as appropriate to the nature and size of the library, fire and emergency protection, physical barrier and lock and key protection, security staff protection, personal access and parcel control protection and security alarms and electronics protection.

v) Auditing the library's assets and its protection systems on a regular basis. When possible such audits should be conducted by security professionals independent of the library with no product or service-related bias.

Foreseeability of Loss

The library director, or designee in safety and security matters, should be responsible for:

i) Anticipating and taking measures to prevent predictable losses such as minor vandalism, injuries, theft of library materials or library user property, utility interruptions, and the non-return of items borrowed from the collection.

ii) Anticipating and taking measures to mitigate catastrophic losses that occur during emergencies and natural disasters, such as earthquakes, major fires or floods, major structural, medical and chemical accidents, weather-related catastrophes, and those from civil unrest, drawing upon local and regional experience as a means of loss avoidance. As the library develops strategies and programmes for security it should examine the experiences and responses of neighbouring institutions who have come to grips with some of these issues. Law enforcement, fire service, risk management, insurance professionals, and others with expertise in loss prevention also should be consulted as appropriate.

iii) Working closely with agencies responsible for recruitment and appointment of personnel to ensure that staff and professional employees have received verification of their identity and past history, avoiding, where possible, any potential threat to other staff, the public, the collections, or other building contents.

iv) Documenting all losses, including from fires, natural disasters, crimes, antisocial behaviour, etc., that occur on or near the library involving employees, library users, their property or library property. This information should be collected and organised in a manner that facilitates the anticipation and prevention of further losses.

v) Maintaining communication with theft reporting media, particularly electronic distribution lists dealing with library loss prevention, security, and stolen property reporting as a means of avoiding the purchase of stolen property and of keeping abreast of security trends and issues.

vi) Reporting promptly any obvious losses to appropriate external agencies to increase the possibility of recovery, to promote the apprehension and punishment of the perpetrator(s), and to help other libraries avoid similar losses.

vii) Seeking professional external evaluation of any high threat sites within the library and any collections, furnishings, or equipment with unusually high value in order to anticipate and prevent security programme inadequacies.

Adequacy of Protection

The library director, or designee in safety and security matters, should be responsible for:

i) Managing situations of gravity and sensitivity and to provide clear and direct emergency direction.

ii) Preparing a library security policy that includes staff rules to protect people, collections, facilities and grounds, and that applies to everyone regardless of position, rank, title, status, or similar reason.

iii) Developing an internal security plan for protection of staff, workers, and patrons.

iv) Evaluating threats against persons and the library to develop effective protection programmes with goals, objectives, timetables, and benchmarks to counter specific threats such as fire, theft, vandalism and mutilation, and personal safety.

v) Preparing and keeping current a library fire evacuation plan and an emergency disaster plan for each library with specific staff instructions and directions, including emergency closing and evacuating, staff notification, life safety responsibilities, maintenance of building integrity and utilities, library stand-alone procedures, and emergency conservation and recovery.

vi) Preparing a security operations manual for routine, operational and emergency situations, which is especially useful during the absence of higher level managers.

vii) Integrating similar facilities and protection duties for background checks; facility and grounds management; emergency liaison with the Federal Emergency Management Administration and other emergency agencies; library strategic planning and construction, and government inspection and reporting for the Occupational Safety and Health Act and the American with Disabilities Act.

Fire and Emergency Protection

The library director, or designee in safety and security matters, should be responsible for:

i) Integrating a fire and emergency protection programme into a library protection policy to avoid and mitigate losses to the library. Fire risk is the major threat to libraries and archives and library protection should be managed accordingly, following the guidance of National Fire Protection Administration (NFPA) National standards, especially NFPA Standard 910 on libraries and library collections, and NFPA Standard 909 for the protection of cultural resources, and subsequent revisions. Each state and city may have fire codes, additional or slightly different from NFPA standards which can be easily verified with the local fire department.

ii) Using reliable early warning fire detection and annunciation systems that are both visual in the form of a strobe light and audible by a bell or horn, with signals clear and distinguishable from other signals and easily understood by all users of the library, including persons with disabilities. The systems must comply with NFPA Standards 71 And 72 and its equipment must be approved by Underwriters' Laboratories (UL), Factory Mutual (FM) or similar nationally recognised testing agencies.

iii) Requiring sufficient exits and exiting guidelines, including areas of rescue assistance, following NFPA Standard 101 on life safety, from the ADA. When a building is occupied an exit shall not be locked preventing its use, obstructed or in any way made unusable. If doors are equipped with electronic/magnetic devices they must release in a fire evacuation situation or loss of power.

iv) Requiring a fire service physical inspection of the library to plan its tactical response, verify the library's compliance with local and state fire codes, and review the library's use of fire prevention practices such as control of the use of open flames. A fire service should also inspect electrical appliances before use including the use of timers with heat generating appliances and check compliance with fire service room occupancy limits.

v) Publishing a library evacuation plan and displaying emergency existing diagrams and instructions for staff and patrons, including persons with disabilities, with a minimum of one fire drill existing per year, in which the staff fully participate.

vi) Ensuring that fire detection systems are monitored continuously at a separately located station such as the municipal police or fire station and a library monitoring centre. Appropriate NFPA Standards such as NFPA Standard 71 and 72 should be followed, using equipment that is approved, and is periodically inspected and recertified by UL. If an uncertified monitoring facility must be used because of local necessity it should be done only with the approval of the local security and fire protection authorities, with regular on-site inspections for its adequacy.

vii) Installing fire service approved fire fighting equipment of an approved kind and quantity, including portable fire extinguishers inspected at least semi-annually and placed in strategic locations throughout the library, following NFPA Standard 10, and when possible water standpipe and hose systems, following NFPA Standard 14. Staff should receive training in the appropriate use of fire extinguishers.

viii) Setting a high priority on protecting the library with an automatic fire suppression system, since libraries hold combustibles and often have structures with open stairwells. A safe, reliable, and often recommended system for libraries and archives in a cross-zoned, wet-pipe water sprinkler extinguishing system specified for minimum sufficient water release, for installation throughout the library, but especially in areas with special risk such as mechanical rooms, kitchens, shops and work spaces using flammables, chemicals and electrical equipment. Automatic fire suppression systems should follow NFPA Standard 11A on medium and high expansion foam systems; NFPA Standard 12 on carbon dioxide extinguishing systems; NFPA Standard 13 on sprinkler systems, and NFPA Standard 17 on dry chemical extinguishing systems.

ix) Planning an effective physical layout of the library with fire walls and doors and the use of automatic door closures following NFPA Standard 101 on life safety and fire dampers and fan shutoffs in ducts to prevent the spread of fire and smoke throughout the library, following NFPA Standard 90A, for air conditioning and ventilating systems, to include an efficient means to ventilate smoke and toxic gases created by fire. Raise awareness with staff and patrons to ensure closure of fire doors to contain a fire situation from spreading.

x) Requiring regular inspection and testing of fire detection, annunciation, suppression and fire fighting systems following appropriate NFPA standards, local fire service codes and equipment recommendations, whichever is more stringent. These include NFPA Standard 13A on the inspection, testing and maintenance of sprinkler systems and NFPA Standard 72H on testing protection signalling systems.

Physical Barrier and Lock and Key Security

The library director, or designee in safety and security matters, should be responsible for:

i) Integrating a physical barrier and lock and key security and/or card system programme into a library protection policy that requires adequate and regular use of physical security closing and locking devices and sound lock and key accountability.

ii) Employing perimeter protection, not leaving external library, non-public, or high value perimeters open or unprotected, nor permitting a contractor to do the same. Adequate operable closure hardware for doors, windows, hatches, gates and cabinets, especially locks, should be furnished. The director should match the relative security of devices and carriers, including balancing the relative protection afforded indoor openings by the door, doorframe, hinges and lock.

iii) Preferring physical perimeter barriers to electronic or staff security checks, closing unused or unnecessary doors, windows, and other exits. While programmable access control systems with digital keypads or cards or biometric readers are encouraged, these and alarms are not adequate physical security by themselves.

iv) Securing high security perimeters with solid surfaces and high security closures on its openings. High security perimeters are perimeters holding special collection storage and other high value objects and the library perimeter, which includes above and below ground level, the roof, open balconies, and atriums.

v) Using good quality, pick resistant dead-bolt locks, on high security perimeters, which use keys whose blanks are not commonly available from locksmiths without a registered signature. Door, window, or hatch hinges and installation nuts or screws for high security hardware should be secured and located on the protected side of the opening. Key openings on the external side of high security perimeter doors, that are not needed for operations, should be fuse closed in order to deny their use by lock picks and unauthorised keys. Exterior windows should use pins or locks not easily opened by breaking panes of glass without detection, nor cam locks as the major device. Sliding glass windows should use double cylinder dead-bolt locks, not thumb turn locks. Double doors and double hung windows may require reinforcement with bars, posts and pins.

vi) Requiring exhibit cases to be firmly constructed or fixed to the wall to avoid easy entry. Use of security screws and brackets, hangers with locking devices or other similar methods that require a knowledge of the attachment systems and time to remove them, should be used. Cam locks, except high security types, should not be used for display cases.

vii) Requiring an effective key and/or cardkey programme, as part of the access control programme, for accountability, control, and strong physical security. This should be planned and operated by one person, preferably closely allied with security operations.

viii) Requiring all keys and/or cardkeys to high security areas to be issued, signed for and returned daily to security where they should be stored in an adequately locked container in the library and accounted for each night.

ix) Accounting for, keeping written record of, and having physical control of keys and/or cardkeys not issued and key blanks.

x) Limiting key and/or cardkey abuse by not issuing keys or cardkeys with bit codes or room numbers to be marked on them. Any contracted locksmith should be bonded.

Security Duties and Security Staff

The library director, or designee in safety and security matters, should be responsible for:

i) Integrating a security programme into the library protection policy for all staff in the library in order to provide security monitoring of conditions. Staff security should include self-protection, protection of immediate responsibilities, surroundings and property, and minor additional security duties when there are no full-time security staff. Libraries with designated security officers should continue this practice even when the library director or security manager employs security officers, referred to here as staff assigned primary security duties.

ii) Requiring all staff to protect themselves and their immediate property and take action when necessary to protect lives and property and report any difficulties for quick correction. All staff should be required to fulfil basic security duties such as being aware of who is in their work areas, following routine security procedures for staff and property, reinforcing patron rules of decorum, keeping valuables out of sight if not locked up, completing first-person opening and last-person closing procedures, and following emergency instructions.

iii) Providing sufficient security staff as staff with primary security duties, at all times that the building is occupied under the direction of a security manager, when there are significant general or specific threats and risks to persons, collections or the library, protect them safely and continue operations. Sufficient staffing includes consideration of adequate security coverage during breaks, shift changes, illnesses, days off, weekends, holidays, and other absences.

iv) Requiring persons assigned to positions with primary security duties to be physically and mentally fit to perform in that capacity.

v) Requiring staff with primary security duties to be responsible for security, including good customer service to patrons and staff, protection of life and property, fair rule enforcement, completion of all fair orders and instructions, staying on duty until relieved in the absence of superiors, and the coordination of emergencies of the library.

vi) Providing staff assigned primary security duties with a procedures manual and sufficient training, including post or patrol assignment security responsibilities, the handling of patron and staff problems and complaints, the handling of library and protection equipment, and the handling of violence and emergencies, especially during the absence of high level managers. The minimum training for security should be one day of classroom instruction prior to working and continuing on-the-job training by a competent and experienced instructor, time and staff trained.

Personal Access and Parcel Control

The library director, or designee in safety and security matters, should be responsible for:

i) Integrating a personal access and parcel control programme into the library protection policy in order to protect lives and assets at the library. It should use physical barriers, entry/exit control devices, and security staff checks and should include everyone using the library, including staff of every category, board members, volunteers, contract and construction workers, interns, researchers, maintenance staff and office visitors, without excepting any library user from security controls. The personal access programme shall define controlled areas by geography and by time, such as secured areas of high value continuously; establish the limits and conditions for their entry and use, including by time and day of week; and establish a means for staff to gain access to those areas to carry out their duties.

ii) Requiring those staff who have been prepared to perform basic security functions to identify and determine the authority or purpose of persons before permitting persons to cross secured library perimeters. As a minimum, the security staff should protect the perimeter for entering and leaving non-public areas and high security areas during open hours.

iii) Requiring the security staff to maintain and use security registers to record consistently the entries and departure of visitors to non-public areas and to all areas during non -public hours. Security staff should use these or similar registers to record also the issue and return of visitor badges, after-hours entry and departure for everyone, and the removal of property from the library and grounds. Contractors and construction staff should be required to comply with this system or be segregated from library areas.

iv) Providing its staff a symbol of authorised access with some visible form of identity such as a name plate, emblem, uniform, or badge to reassure patrons of a staff presence and discourage patrons from imitating the work privileges and behaviours of staff. Security staff should issue a one-time entry badge or authorisation card for visitors to non-public areas, with requirements to comply with visiting rules and be escorted during visits to high security areas.

v) Requiring staff to wear a staff photo identification badge or card visibly to permit easy and safe recognition for entry and work of trusted staff when visibly worn in non-public areas and in all areas of property from the library or grounds. A good photo identification badge or card system should be no smaller than two inches by three and a half inches in size which is laminated or otherwise protected from tampering or forgery and includes the name of the library, a reasonable photo, the person's full name, a register number and/or colour identifying the staff function and a date of expiration.

vi) Limiting and controlling access to secured areas containing sensitive and high value materials such as areas with special collections, negotiables, and sensitive records. Visitors should be limited by means such as registry, key issue, alarms, and/or security escort entry requirements. Visitors should positively identify themselves, demonstrate a clear need to visit there, sign in and out, and be personally escorted by security staff or qualified professional staff. Security should require a ratio of one security escort for every 10 persons when groups visit.

vii) Limiting and controlling object entry, if desirable and feasible, to prevent dangerous and unwanted objects from entering and exit, to prevent illegally or inappropriately obtained materials from leaving. The library director should require staff with primary security duties to perform visual and physical inspection of all materials entering and leaving.

viii) Requiring all library materials being removed from the library to be documented at the check-out desk, as a loan.

ix) Requiring a staff person with primary security duties to review regularly the safety of incoming mail and the security of outgoing mail, including parcels left at the door for pick-up or drop-off.

Security Alarms and Electronics

Security systems require local alarm annunciation when an area is occupied; consistent and rapid human response; professional selection and application of alarm sensors for good alarm coverage; secured communication lines and a backup power supply; appropriate adjusting, testing, inspection and maintenance; and a back-up annunciation at a commercial alarm monitoring facility.

The library director, or designee in safety and security matters, should be responsible for:

i) Integrating electronic intrusion detection and security signalling systems into the duties of security staff in order to provide improved security monitoring of conditions. When no security staff is available, instruct library staff in its proper use to maximise its effectiveness.

ii) Using security alarms to provide continuous alarm protection to some areas and interrupted schedule alarm protection coverage to other areas. Alarm systems in high security areas should have an overlapping security protection with other alarms and a backup alarm annunciation at another location or reporting of alarm to a central station that is monitored 24 hours a day.

iii) Responding to every security alarm annunciation consistently and rapidly. Every local alarm annunciation should be both audible and visual. When the library is closed and empty, the library director shall require the security manager, contract the security company, or the local police to make a consistent and rapid response to every security alarm. The person or company responding to each alarm should report each occurrence and the results of the alarm investigation in writing to the library director.

iv) Fully alarming all library exterior perimeter openings, including high and low areas. All exterior doors, ducts, hatches, and windows which open should use magnetic contact or micro switches to alert the alarm monitoring station of an unauthorised opening. Alarms should be installed on the inside or protected side of the opening. Perimeter exterior surfaces with glass, including doors, panels, skylights and windows in window wells, should use glass break detecting sensors that annunciate when the glass is broken or volumetric motion detection to detect the intrusion.

v) Using volumetric motion detection sensors when possible at strategic places throughout the library during closed hours to detect the unauthorised movement of persons and to detect persons using the library after hours. Some sensors should be visible and some be difficult or impossible to detect. Some should be combination detectors in order to reduce the number of false alarms.

vi) Carefully selecting alarms for object and room protection, especially where high value or high risk materials are kept. Special collection storage rooms and walk-in vaults where high value objects are kept should remain continuously locked and alarmed with magnetic contact or micro switches on all openings; be equipped with vibrator alarm sensors on all flat surfaces to detect forced entry from unprotected areas, and should use motion detection or equal protection inside large areas. Microdot tags and similar radio frequency (RF) field labels using exit detectors should be embedded in high risk library and archive materials. Safes and vaults which contain high values should be located inside secured areas and alarmed with an effective kind of sensor when opened without authority.

vii) Using closed circuit television (CCTV) security monitoring systems when the person watching the monitor has a very high opportunity consistently to notice a problem situation or condition that requires security attention or when an automated CCTV system records that problem situation or condition. CCTV can be considered to assist in verifying staff entering secured perimeters, including with a buzz in; verifying library or alarm conditions; observing readers using high value materials; and detecting the unusual or critical presence of persons or animals in an area that may require attention or response.

viii) Activating or deactivating all or certain alarms at the beginning and end of times of library shutdown (e.g., nights, weekends, holidays, and closed seasons). Staff who open and close facilities should be authenticated by using an alarm keypad with a confidential code or similar means. These persons and those facing a special threat or excessive fear should be protected from takeover by a silent duress/panic alarm.

ix) Installing hard wiring alarm systems whenever possible. Where this is not practical, wireless should be used and supervised in order to (i) signal when batteries become discharged below a minimum power level and (ii) require the control panel to poll or check the detectors at least one per hour or more frequently, as UL standards require.

x) Using a secure alarm monitoring facility that follows UL Standard 1610, central station burglar alarm units and meets Grade AA equipment listing requirements, for protection against compromise or tampering. A compromise is the disconnection of the protected area from the communication line or that from alarm monitoring facility without initiating an alarm signal at the alarm monitoring facility or prevents the transmission of an emergency signal or request for assistance. As a minimum, a panic alarm or secure UL Grade AA Communications link to an outside alarm monitoring facility should be maintained. Any alarm communications link less than a UL Grade AA is considered less protective and should be commissioned as an alternate acceptable means of alarm line supervision by a professional security consultant and by the library director.

xi) Monitoring security alarm lines against tampering with signalling, supervising the circuit to detect any line alterations and making it capable of operating during a power failure for minimum of 24 or longer on batteries, alternative power supplies, generators or other means, or longer if local conditions require.

xii) Requiring appropriate adjusting, testing, inspection and maintenance of the security alarm coverage and services, with various testing to be continuous and ongoing. Maladjusted, malpositioned and untested alarm sensors do not protect.

xiii) Using a back-up annunciation system at a commercial alarm monitoring facility or, where jurisdiction permits, at a municipal police or similar emergency dispatch station. The alarm monitoring facility should follow UL Standard 1610 for central station burglar alarm units and meet Grade AA equipment listing requirements for protection against tampering and compromise. Libraries with highly trained and adequately equipped full-time professional security staffs should consider establishing their own proprietary alarm monitoring facility within a secured area of the library in order to provide better security with more alarm backup, flexibility and monitoring.

Pre-Employment Screening Guidelines

The library director should manage the conduct of background checks as part of an internal security plan that is integrated into the library protection policy for the protection of staff, workers and patrons. He/she should require all library staff applicants and appointees to complete all basic application requests honestly and completely, with final acceptance dependent upon the completion and acceptability—a written job application that accounts for all periods of employment and gaps between employment during the past five years, to ensure that the applicant not avoid including any incarceration, hospitalisation, employment termination or other relevant condition. Applicants who submit incomplete or dishonest materials should be given one opportunity to correct their information. Those who misrepresent or avoid questionable information should require further investigation for final acceptance, to determine whether this behaviour would continue while employed at the library.

A personal interview by a responsible interviewer is a must at the professional level. The interview should double check that the materials submitted belong to the person being interviewed and were completed by that person. Skilled interviewers should note behaviours that may indicate unusual nervousness, incompleteness or deception about any data or issue that merit further investigation.

Licence checks show the library's intention to verify work-related skills and work histories, and an educational achievement check shows the library's correctness to award a work position based on academic achievements. A driver's licence check should indicate if the applicant had a major health, drug or alcohol abuse problem that interfered with operating a vehicle safely and a crafts or guard license or certification check, including union card check, should indicate if the applicant has legitimate work qualifications and a length of satisfactory work in the field. The library director should evaluate each staff position for vulnerability that a person in that position presents to the library, to staff and to patrons, and establish a corresponding level of background check to balance that vulnerability.

Three category levels that is a suggestion for all readers are given below.

i) *Basic level background check*: Designed for staff with little or no access to special collections, patrons, valuables, sensitive information or the management of negotiables.

ii) *Intermediate level background check*: Designed for staff with typical access to collections and patrons but little or no access to valuables, sensitive information or the management of negotiables. This is typical staff access to the library during public and office hours and non-staff visitors with a similar capacity. These persons may move through the collection areas unattended before public hours or before offices close, without access to special collection or high security storage. They do not manage special collection materials or valuables, do not have high security keys, do not have after-hours access and are not assigned in a regular public contact role that may place a patron or the library in jeopardy.

iii) *Advanced level check*: Designed for staff with a level of access that poses a higher potential risk, with regular access to special collections, patrons, valuables, sensitive information or the management of negotiables. This includes staff with primary security duties; mail room, loading dock and shipping and receiving staff; those with sensitive information, especially computer information and computer programming; cashiers and cash handlers, accounting and purchasing staff; and staff with access to special collection storage, high security areas and high security keys.

Advanced level staff checks also require:

a) A reference from all previous employers in the past 10 years and a criminal conviction history check for a period of no less than five years prior to the date of application or as fare back as is legal in the jurisdiction. Note the intermediate entry above for criminal conviction checks and the previous employer check note from the basic application check.

b) A minimum of three references in addition to those previously provided by the applicant, obtained during an interview with the applicant. Note the entry on references above and that the sooner the check may be conducted after receiving the references during the interview, the more valid it may be.

c) A consumer credit check to determine the applicant's credit history. Note that credit and payment histories reveal financial responsibilities and pressures, personal habits and lifestyles that reinforce an understanding of the applicant's character and possible motivation or predisposition to theft or other spending habits.

d) A civil records check to reveal any unreported civil actions that may reflect on the library. Note that permission is required and that a number of different jurisdictions for places of work and places of residence may require inquiries.

e) Verification of the educational achievements claimed by the applicant. Note that distinguished staff are given privileged status at the library and are publicly known for their academic standing on the basis of education achievements that should be verified.

f) A photograph and fingerprints to certify personal identity. Note that fingerprinting requires the taking of good prints and does not require a fingerprint check at the time of hiring. A photograph from the photo identification card process is sufficient.

All persons managing background checks and investigations undergo advance background checks known as a full field investigation, to be conducted and analysed by a professional consultant or local police officials, not by staff from an umbrella organisation who may have concerns or controls that may affect the data or the outcome.

The person or persons conducting these investigations need simply to report the result of the investigation against the advanced level acceptance standards above, keeping the information permanently on file. No one involved in the background check process at the library is exempt form it.

Persons responsible for security should gather, review and maintain the required background information in professional and confidential manner and summarise, report and recommend through the personnel director to the library director, most confidentially, a final opinion for each applicant. The library director should make a decision with the security director and personnel director for final acceptance for employment. Those making final acceptability judgements should link discrepancies in background checks with potential vulnerabilities at the library and make judgements within local law and good ethical judgement. The library director should depend upon the security manager and personnel manager to advocate the best from their professional positions.

Applicants with felony records within the recent past, especially for any form of theft and individuals with arrests for use of illegal drugs or narcotics, should be considered subject to denial of final acceptance for intermediate and advanced level access when they have access to high value records and information. Applicants with a record of serious sexual and child abuse convictions should be considered subject to denial of final acceptance for intermediate and advanced level access when they may work closely with patrons and staff. Applicants with older records of criminal or civil convictions or bad credit history may indicate potential risk but not necessarily dishonesty and may consider the possibility of the applicant to reform.

Staff who manage and process background information should refrain from gathering and refuse to records, report or store information that is irrelevant or immaterial to deciding the final acceptability of the applicant, such as material that is legally discriminatory and court records for civil disobedience involving moral turpitude, sexual preference or similarly irrelevant data.

Exemptions from undergoing background checks and requiring a positive final acceptance are strongly discouraged but inevitably necessary when information and records are incomplete and decisions must be made. No staff should be exempt from the appropriate, predetermined level of background check nor any decision postponed for an inordinate length of time. No staff should be exempt from preparing an application or providing a release to authorise a background check.

Library managers should avoid exempting persons with high status who may present serious vulnerability to the library, including well-known scholars, management and board members and those with high public and professional reputation or standing. When certain records and information are unavailable to investigators, they may gather and use as optional information:

a) A personality profile test, where legal, that is professionally recognised, to determine an applicant's attitude toward honesty, drug use and similar matters.

b) A physical examination with drug test, where legal, and properly administered, to determine the applicant's freedom from medical illnesses and drug or alcohol abuse.

c) A worker's compensation check, where legal, may identify applicants who have left previous staffs after committing insurance fraud.

Background check information as personal information, should be protected in use and in storage, with limited access under high security.

3

Public Safety in Libraries

Most people's mental concept of a library does not entail jarring images of violence, risk, danger, fear, or anxiety or they'd never show up at all. Libraries are normally perceived as tranquil places, where one may spend quiet hours in contemplation and study, and may feel free to find—or lose—one's way. Demonstrably, however, library staff and patrons are increasingly at risk. Crimes committed in libraries are isolated incidents, and libraries are normally safe, secure places both to work in and visit. However, while safekeeping of a library's collection and equipment is obviously very important, personal safety is even more important, for the lives of staff and patrons may be at stake.

Security precautions are necessary and should be considered as part of the price to be paid for working with people. Such precautions may be annoying and will often slow down procedures, but all staff and patrons must be made to see that the precautions are for their benefit, and that without the precautions, they would be more at risk and vulnerable. Unfortunately, in this imprecise and often risky world, there is no such thing as absolute library security.

Librarians and library staff can never have an absolute lock on personal safety for their patrons or staffs, but there are still ways to increase the odds of deterring or preventing incidents. There is a basic trade-off between individual liberties and restricted access to information. In addition to posing restrictions on personal freedoms, such a trade-off involves choices between what we can do to deter crime and the demands such measures make on the library's budget, normally stretched thin enough as it is. This also means a trade-off between money spent on library services and materials and the growing share of the budget that goes to protecting people and materials.

Over the last two decades, library literature has contained numerous stories dealing entirely or in part with safety and security concerns of those who work in, manage, or visit libraries. Taken out of context, such anecdotal evidence could create in the reader's mind a frightening mosaic of risk, peril, and danger. Libraries are not places where one may feel safe to spend one's energies on the intellectual or recreational tasks at hand without undue concern for personal safety. Perhaps the situation is analogous to reading an isolated clipping concerned with an air travel disaster and concluding that getting on a plane is so risky as to be tantamount to suicide.

Publicity is all a matter of scale. Some people live in abject terror of flying because of well-publicised tragedies that occupy the front page of every newspaper for weeks after every airliner tragedy. They prefer to make their way more slowly by using ground transportation. They infer from lurid accounts of such incidents that they happen all the time. And just as people fear being in airliner crashes because every time one falls out of the sky it's a page-one story and the lead item on every television newscast, so library crimes tend to be long remembered because they are so rare and thus so widely publicised. Yet one does not read very much about security-related incidents of crime in libraries precisely because incidents of trouble are so rare.

In the sense of removing library materials without following procedures, or keeping them beyond their borrowing period, the public is occasionally guilty of crimes or at least misdemeanours. But if one considers physical or violent crime in the library, the magnitude of the offence is much greater, and the transgressor is normally a member of one of the following four categories of people:

i) Patrons disgruntled or enraged with library policies or with staff members' attitude or behaviour.

ii) Persons with irrational behaviours, mental probiems, domestic disturbances, sometimes augmented and exacerbated by drug or alcohol abuse.

iii) Former employees, seething with resentment and looking for a payback for being demoted, passed over for promotion, fired, or downsized.

iv) Criminals with or without weapons intending to use violence to achieve their goals.

Every library must take steps to create a safe environment for staff and patrons. While no library or institution of any size is immune to threats, prevention of most violent events or threats is possible with careful planning and cooperation from employees.

Library buildings are no more immune to violence than other public facilities. In fact, their unique characteristics may actually invite or create a favourable environment for violence:

a) They are normally the only public buildings open evenings and weekends, and that fact attracts people who have no place else to go.

b) Few libraries have metal detectors installed at the front doors, and little ability to search visitors.

c) Many libraries cannot afford security staff or off-duty police officers on-site. In the absence of such controls, criminals feel free to do whatever they like.

d) Evening staff also have to deal with patrons leaving the library late at closing time, knowing that they must follow the patrons out 10 minutes later.

All public and most academic libraries are intentionally open to all who seek to enter them—which constitutes both the best and worst feature of the institution. That is, the best thing about the library is that anyone—regardless of race, creed, age, gender, ethnicity, wherewithal, stated or unstated reason for the visit, property ownership, or identification—may enter and partake of the services and collections. At the same time, the sheer extent of that freedom can be the worst thing about the library, because not everyone who enters does so with the intent of using the building, its facilities, and its materials for accepted, library-related purposes.

In fact, many public libraries have become—if not by charter, then by custom and usage—magnets for the troubled, havens for the homeless, and social gathering places for legitimate and illegitimate activities. The public library is commonly seen as a place that welcomes all corners and cannot legitimately turn them away, so long as they refrain from objectionable behaviour, do not snore while they sleep, and fake it well enough to look as if they are reading when someone observes them.

Even severely offensive personal odour or lack of a permanent address do not seem to be universal criteria for exclusion or expulsion, as recent court cases have proved. Yet, because of this very openness, libraries may be frequented by thieves, vandals, disturbers of the peace, drug users and vendors, firebugs, sexual deviates, the mentally ill, and all those with a nasty attitude they want to take out on the world. And while the vast preponderance of a library's problem patrons are not bent on harm or destruction of human life, many of them visit the library only to pry upon and destroy the collections.

A behaviour policy provides guidelines for determining and managing unacceptable behaviour. It protects library patrons and staff from abusive actions of others that undermine the purpose of the library. If it's done right, such a policy is at the same time easy to understand, consistent, equitable, and fair. Having a written policy also provides safety and security officials with the authority to intervene when called to the library, and it may be used as a reference document when individuals challenge rules or seek to fight their expulsion. The purpose of such a policy is to ensure that all problem behaviours are defined and lawfully prohibited, with subsequent actions and reactions prescribed.

Specific issues to be addressed in such a policy will vary with the library's circumstances, and can be facilitated by consulting staff, campus police, and other officials, and by examining other libraries' successful policies and procedures. Problem behaviours may reasonably be divided, according to the severity of the activity, into two broad classes: threatening and non-threatening. It would be nice if there was a clear-cut line of demarcation between those categories. However, since the distinction between them is frequently blurred, a beleaguered or highly stressed staff member may guess wrong about which is which, or a given individual may be both at the same time, or first one and then the other, as a confrontation escalates.

i) *Nuisances / non-threatening behaviours*:

— beggars

— hustlers and freelance salespersons

— idlers, loafers, loiterers, and vagrants

— drunks

— eaters, snackers

— finger tappers

— laughers, loud talkers, loud yawners

— coughers, wheezers, singers, hummers, sleepers

— hyperactives

— loud whisperers

— persons who appear to be talking to themselves

— pet owners who bring animals into the library

— malodorous but otherwise innocuous persons

— monopolisers of staff time
— lonely seniors desperately craving for human contact
— mutilators and defacers of library property
— censors who seek to remove objectionable parts from books or magazines
— moralists, preachers, and proselytisers
— voyeurs, starers
— public telephone monopolizers
— thieves and pickpockets
— compulsive rearrangers and tidiers
— latchkey children with nowhere else to go
— persons seeking consensual sexual contact
— practical jokers
— rule breakers
— the homeless.

While all the listed behaviours can be extremely annoying, most of the individuals committing them in the library can safely be dealt with by unarmed staff members, even if all such people cannot necessarily be considered harmless, and thus worthy of being either indulged or overlooked.

ii) *Behaviours that pose a serious and real threat to staff and other patrons*:
— drug sellers, buyers, and users
— fighters and those looking to pick quarrels with others angry or aggressive people
— delinquents, who may or may not be gang members
— the mentally disturbed
— weapon carriers
— sexual deviants or sexual predators
— exhibitionists

— verbal abusers
— persons who use profanity aloud
— arsonists
— extortionists
— vandals
— child molesters and paedophiles
— touchers
— fetishists
— paranoids, who may also be schizophrenics
— those who use public rooms or telephones to conduct illegal business dealings.

Even when a person may be classified as belonging to the latter category, a clear sense of what to do about his or her behaviour is not always obvious, or even agreed upon. Most problem patrons are of the non-violent variety, and, however annoying they may be, will not commit violent acts on others. Library staff members should become a little paranoid, perhaps, and learn to watch everybody for problem behaviours. As a preliminary step, they should first anticipate problems with the public by attempting to define and ban or deal within a recommended way specific problem behaviours, and to post their lists of prohibitions prominently.

There are people frequenting libraries every day, seemingly for the obvious purpose of following young women around or otherwise terrorising fellow visitors. Once undesirable activities are suspected, patrollers are able to observe and follow these people, to deter, to observe and report their objectionable behaviours.

Local police or campus security may be called in to deal directly with these individuals based on staff security members' observations. On occasion, these people may be officially barred from the library, or even from a college campus. But almost inevitably, most show up in the library again, often within hours of their exile. In these instances, security staff have the duty of making quick identification of these recidivist problem patrons and the obligation to monitor their behaviour until the police come to intervene. Unless it is a clear case, easily determined to be a police issue, we should carefully examine each situation before determining that a problem patron is in our midst.

PROBLEMS FORM HOMELESS PERSONS

Many homeless persons, with no place else to spend their time, find the library a more comfortable ambiance for their daytime hours than the streets, and a much more affordable one than any other spot in town. While homeless persons in the library may present severe problems, they are patrons of the library, and should be treated to the extent possible like everyone else who enters the building.

Similarly, they are subject to the same rules and regulations as are persons with homes. In keeping with both law and tradition, homeless people, regardless of their degree of personal hygiene, receive the protection of the First and Fourteenth Amendments to the US Constitution, just as do the methodist minister, the mayor's wife, and the high school girls doing their homework after school. In other words, as long as they are violating no established building or municipal rules, the homeless are not eligible for eviction.

In times of homelessness, people with nowhere else to go naturally gravitate to public buildings as a haven from the streets. These places offer warmth, shelter, public rest rooms, and quiet rooms where one can read, socialise, and, on occasion, sleep without the requirement of paying for the privilege or worrying about being assaulted or robbed. Along with homelessness, of course, come other related problems, stemming from lack of access to or interest in proper sanitation and hygiene, and, due to economic and societal problems, mental illness. All of these worries affect the library directly, of course, as well as all who spend time in it.

As homelessness is a great social and personal tragedy, the consequences and ramifications for libraries are immense. The homeless generally fall into the amorphous library classification of problem patrons, along with thieves, exhibitionists, and persons whose behaviours are annoying and worrisome, yet completely legal. It is, however, important to remember that not all homeless persons are problem patrons, and correspondingly, not all problem patrons are homeless.

The library is tops on the short list of places for the homeless to go. In every city, down-town commercial buildings have security personnel whose routine responsibilities include that of shooing away undesirables. The homeless obviously vary in their potential for problem behaviour, and library staff and security personnel are frequently required to make impromptu and subjective distinctions among such poorly defined terms as eccentric, highly emotional, emotionally disturbed, and even psychotic. In the absence of on-site and immediate psychiatric evaluation of individuals, in fact, most such classifications become nothing more than snap judgment calls, which will accordingly vary with the individual observer.

Homeless people cannot be classed as a monolithic entity. Just as they are unique in their appearance, they do not all act, react, or think the same way. Some are, admittedly, seriously and dangerously ill, and that illness may be physical, mental, or emotional. They may be drunks or substance abusers or clean and sober. Others are quite normal, in the sense of being average in intelligence or perception and free from obvious substance abuse. What they frequently share, however, is a syndrome of conditions from which they cannot easily escape.

Library literature is full of news items concerning the conflicting rights of persons to have free access to library materials and other persons seeking the same access in nontoxic air. The homeless tend to feel suspicion and sometimes anger toward police and social workers, or the variety of people who approach them offering help, seeking to rehabilitate their bodies, their work skills, or, sometimes, their souls. A sense of hopelessness is often pervasive among them, and it takes more than either charity or policy to make that feeling go away.

Through bitter, first-hand experience, the homeless are often disinclined to trust do-gooders beyond accepting charity when it is offered. Many are proud, disdaining charity, and subsisting on only what they can provide for themselves. Others have a talent for panhandling and telling hard-luck stories to affluent passersby or other library patrons, making a surprising income through preying on the generosity, guilt, or discomfort of others. Feeding themselves adequately is often a daylong occupation of the homeless, and alcohol, when available, is both a comfort and an enemy.

The homeless make use of the public library as shelter from the streets; within its walls, they can, depending on the prevailing weather, warm up, cool off, sleep, use clean rest room facilities, and simply spend the day. Some of them actually read or use library materials, while others use those materials as props, as a justification for their presence in the library. Most homeless people feel a sense of entitlement to the library as citizens and former or occasional taxpayers, and see no reason why they should be treated any differently from other visitors to the building.

With a few exceptions, they are meek and inoffensive, knowing that their continued ability to enter and use the building has a good deal to do with their comportment and behaviour. Many, if they could choose, would become transparent or invisible, free to enter and move about the library without attracting the notice of staff, guards, or other patrons. For the most part, homeless patrons must be treated just like those with homes. The library's set of rules for behaviour, demeanour, attire, and personal hygiene must apply to all visitors to the building, regardless of their economic status or residence.

THEFTS

As librarians, mindful of our role as the keepers of memory, we not only recoil but also take it personally when someone attacks or tries to steal items from the collections in our care. Stealing is not only against the law, but it is also condemned as wrong by virtually all societies. The theft of library books is not generally considered to be a serious crime, perhaps because owning books is seen by many people as worthy and intrinsically good, and perhaps because stealing books is sometimes explained as a form of borrowing.

Book theft is seen as distinct from such major crimes as stealing cars or computers, despite the fact that a single rare book that a skilled thief may take from a library may be worth more individually than a new luxury automobile. Books may be stolen to help the thief achieve economic goals or to further political aims, to rescue the book from abuse at the hands of its uncaring custodians, or just for the sheer joy of possession of something desired.

In some cases, people steal books only to prove that a resourceful thief can defeat the library's pathetic attempts at security. But the end result of all such crime is the same: The book is missing, and no one may any longer consult it or use it. Therefore, all library crime should be taken as equally seriously as shoplifting in commercial establishments, and every person found guilty of library crime should be prosecuted. Successful prosecutions given adroit publicity will not only punish those who attempt to diminish libraries by misappropriating our property, but may serve as a possible deterrent to the next little person with big ideas who sees the library as an opportune cash cow for exploitation. Some may see a rough economic justification for committing such crimes as library book theft.

Sometimes the library thief is just a person who has suffered real or perceived injustice at the hands of society, and community. In such cases, the thief may just feel that he is merely looking for a little payback and getting even. So he grabs a book and walks out, or maybe just defaces one inside the building.

Some library users even make up their own rules, based upon their perception of self-interest. In truth, there are so many worse crimes committed today that book theft hardly seems criminal behaviour to most of us because it pales in comparison with such acts as drive-by murders, serial killings, or rapes. It is just a game for some people, with its own set of low risks and high rewards.

An initial small crime might go so well that the criminal might decide to take it one step further. Taking a stapler or a pack of post-its-home from work or a book out of the library without going through procedures does not necessarily lead down the slippery slope that results in holding up the corner bank or embezzling funds from a company's holdings.

Committing a small crime may be a one-shot event, but for some people, it can actually become addictive and can lead to a destructive major behaviour pattern. Countless case study profiles, thumb-nailing criminal careers in libraries, demonstrate the chronicles of people who started small and then gradually became more ambitious after initial successes.

For the sake of classification and convenience, library thieves may be divided into six basic classes, based on their principal motivation for committing theft. Such people, however, do not necessarily fit the stereotype of what you may think of as a criminal. Library thieves, in fact, frequently turn out to be dean's-list students, distinguished professors, elected public officials, librarians themselves, or just about anybody else, and any of them may fall into two or more of the following classifications:

i) *Bibliokleptomaniacs:* They cannot keep themselves from stealing books. They take books out of a compulsion to do so, and are in need of psychiatric assistance. Such people will usually take good care of the books, and a few will even surreptitiously bring them back at a later time.

ii) *Thieves who steal for their own personal use:* They steal either for the secret pride of possession or to have the materials conveniently handy for consultation. They may feel they have the right to have the books because they pay taxes, tuition, and so on. Most of the time they will take good care of the book because they think of it as theirs.

iii) *Thieves who steal for revenge:* They harbour a real or imagined grievance against the library or someone in a management position, possibly for having been fired. These thieves do what they do because they are looking for payback. Unfortunately, thieves in this class may destroy or deface the materials they have stolen in order to punish the library.

iv) *Casual thieves:* They may steal a book because it is just too time-consuming and bothersome to go through check-out or because they do not have borrowing privileges at the library and are unwilling or unable to arrange for them.

v) *Freelance censors:* They who remove books to keep them out of the hands of others, whether because of disapproval of their contents or fear of the consequences of their being accessed by susceptible readers. Such people may be motivated by the desire to protect innocent persons and the fear that, while they personally can handle strange ideas on sex, politics, religion, or lifestyles without being either depraved or corrupted, others cannot.

vi) *Thieves who steal for profit:* They may be staff members or outsiders who will subsequently attempt to sell the books, and thus can be caught if booksellers are ethical and alert. But the more careful book thieves are meticulous, clever, and unlikely to make mistakes. In this class, the major and most serious predators of library materials do what they do for a living. Often such criminals live as transients, living out of vehicles and preying on libraries and bookstores to support themselves or just to keep in practice, as they wend their way around their region or across the country. Concern has been expressed among law enforcement agents that some crooks may know one another and sometimes work together or otherwise cooperate and/or exchange favours and spoils.

In 1982, the Rare Books and Manuscripts Section (RBMS) of the Association of College and Research Libraries (ACRL) created a Security Committee with the charge to develop and disseminate appropriate guidelines to secure library collections, and to serve as a resource for libraries who have experienced theft, to serve as a liaison with other organisations whose interests are deterring the theft of library materials and vigorously promoting the proper prosecution of library thieves. The committee subsequently published *Guidelines Regarding Thefts in Libraries*, which called for the appointment of Library Security Officers (LSOs), persons with principal responsibility for security on the part of the library, among other things. There is no invariable pattern of criminal behaviour in libraries, but successful thieves have several attributes and behaviours in common:

i) *Surveillance:* They study people, systems, and physical layouts.
ii) *One or more trial runs:* Many thieves caught have later confessed to having walked through the projected crime area several times prior to the actual event, to trouble-shoot any potential difficulties and to assess the library's defences.
iii) *Careful observation:* They look for the weaknesses in the library's defences.

The would be criminals try to find a path of least resistance. Possession of a purloined key is much easier and works better than dynamite or drilling through locks. It is also much simpler to have the key and the code than to try to defeat an alarm system. Key control, therefore, is paramount to a secure library operation. The key thief usually assumes that even if he/she is caught, the worst-case scenario would be being found guilty of a minor infraction of existing laws or rules with little or no punishment. Another assumption made by felons and would-be felons is that libraries do not communicate with one another about the problem of theft, meaning that each library the thief visits is a fresh start, with the staff unaware of both who and what he is. A skilful thief, in fact, can do untold damage to a single library or, like a serial killer, go from place to place committing crimes.

There are various methods that can be and can have been used to gain access to libraries' special collections and steal their books. Stolen keys and picked locks can allow the thief to elude after-hours security systems. Obliteration of property markings, if properly and carefully done, will not only conceal the provenance of a book, but will make the task of figuring out its rightful owner all the harder. To show the extent to which a resourceful thief will go to obliterate the markings of book ownership, book thieves eventually caught have confessed to having done the following:

a) used fictitious library stamps.
b) carried blank, perforated, gummed spine labels, which they affixed to book spines after removing the library's labels and on which they created fictitious call numbers.
c) carried bookplates, book pockets, and date due slips, and pasted them into books to create false identity or to cover up ownership marks.
d) sandpapered library names off spines and edges of books and removed bookplates.
e) cut out or blackened library names in books.
f) befriended and became personally familiar with library staff members, causing them to relax their vigilance and view the thief as a regular.
g) disguised themselves—dressing as everything from disheveled street people to college professors—when attempting to fence their stolen materials to antiques dealers.

h) scaled library walls using mountain-climbing equipment, or in some cases, only fingertips and toeholds in the brick facing.
i) obtained schematics of the libraries' alarm systems and/or floor plans.

While theft, vandalism, and damage are all inevitable in libraries and other public repositories of documents, determined and clever thieves are always going to find new and better ways to make off with their books and other properties. Guardians of both the public and private trust must take all necessary measures to ensure that such threats and dangers to their collections, since they cannot be eliminated, are at least minimised or made much more difficult to pull off.

Librarians admit as much when they refrain from words like 'stolen' and talk about long-overdue books not having been 'returned yet'. They obviously would not be so charitable about the kid who hot-wired their car last night and drove off. The difference between books and cars is that books deal in ideas, and ideas are supposed to be free. The whole idea of theft is to avoid detection, and librarians are reluctant to discuss an embarrassing lack of security, for several reasons. Sometimes, a missing book turns out to be merely misplaced or temporarily stuck in limbo. It is not always easy to distinguish between what is overdue, what is lost in the system, or what is stolen.. Even with imperfect statistics and the reticence of some to talk about the subject, it is still possible to piece together a plausible most-stolen list in somewhat the same way police artists sketch a criminal's face from fragmentary recollections.

The motives of the thieves may vary; some of those accused of major thefts even plead compulsion or insanity at their trials. Other felons claim indignantly that they did their deeds to preserve and protect materials that the city, the county, or the university was doing a poor job of protecting, leaving books and manuscripts vulnerable and requiring rescue by an enlightened saviour. Usually, in a legal context, the issue is whether the defendant, who might be suffering from a mental disability or illness, knows right from wrong.

False identification cards, aliases, open stacks, and staff innocently and unwittingly helping criminals make our libraries too open to theft. Unless we study the motives of those involved in thievery and attempt more effectively to deter theft, our collections will shrink, our patrons will be unhappy, the costs of providing library service to the community will go up unnecessarily, and our potential donors will look elsewhere for secure locations for their bequests. Thieves normally find libraries pleasant places in which to ply their trade. There is nothing to stop them from entering and no barrier to pass or requirement that they stop, show identification, discuss anything, pay an admission charge, or do anything else that might call attention to themselves or cause people to remember them later.

People tend to let their guard or innate wariness down inside a library. The street smarts that serve them well in urban communities are sometimes put aside or deactivated in the sedate and quiet precincts of a library reading room. That represents an opportunity for the clever thief. In fact, the library seems so safe that after the thief strikes, the victim may actually feel betrayed by the library because something was stolen.

Prevention of crime in libraries before they occur would be the best thing, but failing that, deterrence is possible, and in most cases, it begins with attitude adjustment. Some important considerations for prevention of theft of library property includes:

— Theft and loss occur less often when staff use and check existing locks and alarms regularly.
— There is less theft and loss when staff visibly or physically perform inventory regularly.
— Theft and loss are always reduced when staff apply the business principles of risk management to their institution.

— Theft prevention is less expensive than the cost of legal recovery or replacement.
— Missing items are found more often when they are immediately reported as missing.
— Every library should change locks and keys from time to time as a matter of good business practice.
— Regularly examine the basic means you use for protection.
— Private areas of buildings need clear separation and marking from public areas, with locks or control of entry and exit to them.
— To avoid theft and other losses, managers should ask insurance specialists and other protection professionals for advice.
— Theft is best prevented by physically separating valuables from those who would remove them, using non-walk spaces such as pits, platforms, and height before using ropes, railings and glass.
— Theft and loss are often prevented when staff consider looking after the property as if it were their own.
— Some thefts will inevitably occur, but 99 per cent of them are preventable.
— Thefts inevitably occur through carelessness or neglect.
— Thefts from public or government property are viewed as acceptable to some people. The key is to make library thefts appear as thefts from the people or heritage of the country, which may arouse a sense of outrage in a largely indifferent public.
— Employee thefts occur less often when ethics codes are known and respected by all staff.
— Thefts by outside persons are often assisted by staff, even without their knowledge. Be careful with sensitive or security information.
— Theft also includes embezzlement, forgery, misappropriation, extortion, and hijacking.

Most people would not leave book bags, purses, or coats unattended at a restaurant table while they use the rest room or pay their bill, yet many people do just that when using libraries. They leave all sorts of personal belongings alone for just a minute or two while browsing the shelves, using the copiers, rest rooms, telephones, catalogues, and so on. Patrons often seem quite surprised and angry when they find their belongings missing. Staff are entirely within their rights to demand to know who is using the library.

Libraries are also businesses; specifically, the library is in the lending and information business. Like other businesses, we must know how to get in touch with our customers. To qualify for library services, a valid identification card with address and photo may be necessary, and it is reasonable to expect people to produce such documents upon request. People who reside outside the library's governmental jurisdiction or who have no permanent residence could be hard to track down if materials are not returned. Sometimes patrons refuse to provide this information, for a variety of reasons. Signs, brochures, and staff guidelines are necessary, and acceptable behaviour policies are imperative. We must be vigilant and diligent about educating both our public and our staff. This proactive approach will go a long way to cut down on complaints and improve public relations.

Magazines and other periodicals constitute the number one target of opportunity for library thieves. Also high on the petty larceny hit list are such commonly ripped-off materials as automobile repair manuals, newspapers, adult magazines, and sports magazines. Like so many other problems, this is not unique to libraries. Libraries, in fact, are comparative novices in protecting their materials, especially when compared with high-risk private purveyors. There is much librarians could learn, for example, from convenience stores regarding loss.

By one estimate, libraries, regardless of type, are being pillaged of two to five per cent of their book collections annually and five to 25 per cent of their audiovisual collections. The sheer total of loss and destruction of material in various types of physical and electronic collections has grown into a major national and international problem. From a public relations standpoint, such losses are very bad for the library's image as well. There is nothing sadder than having a patron need, something we think we own and being unable to provide it because it is lost, stolen, strayed, missing, or simply unaccounted for.

The illicit removal of physical objects from archives, libraries, museums, and collections has always presented a problem for their owners and guardians, whether they are private individuals or public administrators. Securing material is much easier in a private collection that is completely inaccessible to anyone except the owner than it is in a large library or museum whose very existence is predicated on serving the public. Libraries' responses to materials' disappearance can range from naive laxity or indifference to extraordinary vigilance bordering on paranoia. Most libraries seek to take some middle road between these extremes. This path allows them to avoid continually losing valuable materials, yet prevents their countermeasures from alienating patrons. Among the most popular and affordable security measures is the use of narrow strips of magnetic tape inserted into the spines of print materials.

Tattle-tape was a revolutionary idea when it arrived on the scene many years ago. Thousands of the nation's libraries began putting magnetic devices into books that trip sensors if the volumes are not properly checked out at the loan desk. Thousands of libraries that were financially able scrambled to secure print holdings in this way. Using minimum-wage or student workers, tattling all books could render collections of half a million or more books secured within a matter of weeks. Librarians then figured that they could now relax, since their precious holdings were protected from theft.

However, the security countermeasures eventually meet with new threats. These lead to improved countermeasures and so on in an endless chain. It did not take potential thieves very long to figure out how to beat the tattle-tape system; they did, and still do, *en masse*. Statistics are difficult to obtain to verify the actual security of holdings when tattle-tape is used; libraries are typically if understandably disinclined to discuss their shortcomings. The alarm usually does ring and a waist-high gate may even lock when a patron tries to leave the library with material that has not been desensitised, presumably signalling an attempted theft.

Sometimes, however, the alarm may ring for other reasons, or for no reason at all. Unfortunately, the alarm often rings when a desensitising machine malfunctions. If this happens enough times, staff may simply come to ignore it. Busy workers at counters also make the common error of not desensitising material that has been legitimately checked out, a human error difficult to control or correct. Even if the material has been checked out, and if a functioning desensitising machine has been used appropriately, the alarm may still sound. This can be a traumatic or intensely irritating experience for the conscientious and law-abiding patron who checks out books in the prescribed manner and still sets off the alarm. An ongoing complaint against tattle-tape, in fact, is that it has a surprisingly high error rate. Despite its ubiquitousness, perhaps the most condoned crime in the community and on campus is theft of library materials; this work of unscrupulous or indifferent people is costing libraries millions of dollars yearly.

Theft from libraries may run as high as 20 per cent per year, yet few libraries conduct regularly scheduled inventories because it is boring, labour-intensive, and too costly in staff time. What is more, they make little attempt to identify security problems and often refuse to prosecute those individuals caught in the act. In this sense, we are often our own worst enemies, giving aid and comfort to the potential enemies who would steal from us.

An immediate and inexpensive way to attempt to reduce incidents of theft in libraries is to post simple signs cautioning people to mind their belongings just the way they would do outside the building. This may serve as a reminder to the public, when victims report a purse, a laptop, or a jacket missing. Signage and patron education are both required. We are not responsible for lost or stolen items signs are common, even in coat-check areas of restaurants and other commercial establishments.

Libraries need similar signs to warn and inform people of a potential risk, problem, or condition, and whose responsibility it is when something is stolen. Signs may seem obvious, but they do help remind people of the problem of theft. They further serve to protect the library when problems arise and those who have been ripped off are looking for someone to blame or sue for their losses. Even without talking about the intervention of thieves and vandals, library losses each year are significant due to the natural processes of wear, humidity, heat, ill use or abuse, or just plain aging.

However, in a very real sense, the cumulative effect of theft or mutilation of books or other property from a library is a disaster like an earthquake, a hurricane, or a fire. The result, from the library's standpoint, is very similar—the only difference is one of degree. Books, however, tend to disappear from the library one or two at a time, meaning that, unlike other types of disasters, this one sneaks up quietly and without attracting undue notice. With library budgets being what they are and with the increasing emphasis on serving the public, many libraries never get around to performing any form of inventory. They just resign themselves to living with their losses.

However, the resulting disaster from theft or mutilation may be as devastating as any natural disaster for an institution's collections and staff morale, even if nothing life-threatening occurs. The good library books lead hard but frequently short useful lives. Many disappear, their whereabouts unknown. Others get lost, stolen, or stray. More than a few lose pages are returned minus their front covers.

They develop broken spines, grubby covers, or pages like prune skin, the result of falling into the tub while being read by bathers or being used as shelter during that sudden rainstorm.

Just as water-soaked or smoke-damaged materials caused by a hurricane, flood, or fire are lost forever if timely action is not taken to treat them, so stolen materials are lost forever if timely action is not taken to attempt to recover them. In the process, action must be taken to stop thieves from any future activity. Preventing theft and incorporating attempts at theft prevention into a disaster plan should be ranked with natural disasters as threats to the library's security, the collection's integrity, the community's intellectual heritage, and so on.

The misdeeds of a large number of professional book thieves have come to light. While much of the evidence is anecdotal, certain threads can be woven together to create a profile of the habitual library thief and prevailing *modus operandi*. Despite eternal vigilance, the nation's rare and valuable books are still reported missing at a frightening and depressing rate. For example, you can still read many of the library of Congress's journals of nineteenth-century expeditions and its rare old botanical encyclopedias and bird books. You just cannot see very many of the pictures. Nearly 27,000 valuable maps, engravings, and hand-coloured illustrations have been cut out and, librarians suspect, fenced to unscrupulous or unwitting dealers.

The stolen plates, worth an estimated $1.75 million, are feeding a burgeoning US market in rare prints and engravings. Approximately 300,000 books are missing from LC, according to the latest tally, which accounts for the new, harsher policy of stack admittance now in force. Many of the library's books are rare, old, richly illustrated, and salable. Their loss or mutilation is emblematic of a more general hemorrhage for public, private, university, and governmental libraries, irreplaceable older materials disappear. If a thief is careful, the odds are still pretty good that he/she will not get caught. Some guidelines to slow this bleeding away of from libraries are given below:

i) Treat the library materials with stop-loss preventives, such as indelible property marking if possible. Sometimes a simple property stamp and an ink pad may serve to protect and identify library property and deter those who would steal it.

ii) Security equipment and staff should be a significant part of the library's operating budget.

iii) Security expenditure should be the same proportionately for all libraries. The goal in every case is good security.

iv) Good security for materials also helps to deter nuisance incidents and in-library crime against people.

Library staff may have to disabuse both visitors and staff of the long-standing notion that the library is a safe haven, despite the possibility that awareness of this reality may negatively affect both circulation figures and library visits. Posting a highly visible warning sign to the effect that library users should be vigilant against purse snatchers and other thieves may help remind patrons of inevitable dangers and risks without occasioning undue alarm.

Since many rare book librarians are hesitant about reporting their losses out of embarrassment or fear of frightening donors, other librarians cannot keep up by reading the professional literature. So that we need to publicise and be willing to talk about our losses. If we do not talk to one another, individuals or gangs and occasionally assigning roles to confederates will keep on stealing books and manuscripts and selling them to shady collectors or fences.

Is the primary concern of the library to ensure unlimited access to the library collections or is it to enforce rules such as making the existing collection available on demand, even if that means restrictions on personal liberties within the building? One way to look at the problem, of course, is to embrace the argument that book theft is actually a tribute to the value and utility of libraries and that if no one ever stole or mutilated anything, it would demonstrate the lack of need for libraries. Such a view may offer us a modicum of cold comfort when we finally get around to inventory and discover that we have lost vital chunks of our collection. Security precautions are a price to pay for having material when people want it or need it. Patrons must be made to see that precautions are for their benefit.

Every library director or board should appoint a Library Security Officer (LSO) and establish a Security Planning Group. The LSO and this group should work with the institution's public relations personnel and establish contact with local law enforcement before any problems arise. It is also important to establish contact with local book dealers to alert them to ways to identify stolen materials. If an institution is an academic or independent research library, the name of the LSO should be reported to the ACRL-RBMS Security Committee for inclusion on the LSO list available from the ACRL office. This also makes the library eligible for participation in the LSO distribution list, which reports incidents of theft. It was established in 1994 and is still published by the ACRL-RBMS Security Committee. In reaction to evidence of the deliberate and widespread theft of library materials, some research libraries have taken steps to strengthen their security with the aim of thwarting future Blumbergs.

Some of the better endowed already boast of a state-of-the-art system, designed to thwart and frustrate would-be library thieves. Such a security system would have the following parts:

i) A zoned perimeter and closed-circuit TV system, including an after-hours combination of motion detectors, closed-circuit television (CCTV) monitors, and VCRs, with video display monitors hooked up to CCTV cameras and video recorders, and a video switcher selecting what to display on the monitors.
ii) Emergency fire exit protection at all entrances, which includes magnetic door contacts and a CCTV monitor permanently trained on each exit, with the video camera automatically activated whenever the door is opened.

iii) Halon fire suppression system and water detectors for all special collections areas and vaults.

iv) A fire detection system including sprinklers in all rooms except special collections vaults.

v) A panic button that silently notifies local police or campus security, located on the staff side of the main service desk.

vi) Every desk supplied with a detailed floor plan showing the location of security devices and zones.

vii) Rekeying of the entire library, with employee signatures on file for all keys.

viii) Special collections areas accessed only through locked doors. The outer door is always kept closed unless being used and is locked at closing. The inner door is always locked as well. Entrance is gained by a buzzer answered by a member of the curatorial staff who secures, authenticates, and retains the ID card of the patron until all materials are returned.

One option for libraries is a high degree of tight security such as that boasted by government and military installations, even though many patrons find such measures to be intimidating and highly user-unfriendly.

In order to get serious about security, it would institute the following measures commonly found on active military bases.

— Guards at all access points.
— Photo ID for admission.
— Retinal, fingerprint or voice recognition scanners.
— Passwords for computer use.
— Need-to-know basis for information.
— An authorisation code for use of equipment and materials.
— Public and certain knowledge of penalties.
— Surveillance cameras.

— Intrusion alarms, heat sensors, motion detectors, etc.
— Searching of belongings at exits to the building.

The staff members of libraries universally cringe at the very thought of the tiresome chore of inventory shelf reading. Anyone who has performed this odious task knows just how time-consuming and boring it is. It is still the most effective device in identifying what is missing and which subjects require greater surveillance. Hand in hand with surveillance goes the shelf-list catalogue, which many libraries either poorly maintain or have completely abandoned.

Researchers often find library procedures cumbersome and detrimental to their needs. They become frustrated with tiresome routines and their frustration can result in theft. Professors cue their students about visiting distant libraries. They need to call or write ahead of the visit and alert librarians there concerning the scope of their research.

Libraries need to provide special space and services to serious researchers. Historians have complained of non-existent or inadequate space and of long waits for library staff to locate needed documents. One major library requires 24 hours notice to provide historical material. Researchers complain of being limited to a few items at a time, of having to complete many borrowing forms, of the lack of microfilming or photocopying facilities, and so on. There needs to be a better understanding of the problem of theft by researchers and of the frustrations of busy researchers by librarians.

If we are wishing for a better world, we should protect our collections by creating and enforcing a set of universal rules designed to reduce or even stop library crime. Among these might be the following:

i) Upon entering, a patron presents identification to a security officer. This identification card is retained until the patron leaves the building.

ii) Outside the reference or reading room, all coats, briefcases, notebooks, envelopes, and so on are placed in lockers.

iii) The patron must show and surrender his or her identification card for entry to the reference or reading room if that was not done upon entering the library.

iv) The patron is limited to one box of material or book or folder open at a time.

v) Library staff will be encouraged to walk among library users, actively paying attention to what they are doing and unconcerned with whether they are perceived as being snoops.

vi) After the patron has used protected materials, his or her belongings will be searched.

vii) When exiting the room, the user's identification card is returned by the security officer.[7]

There is normally no unified or consistent security apparatus between libraries or among libraries, booksellers, and law enforcement agencies. E-mail networks have been created for members to communicate and for posting warnings. Closer working relationships between librarians and antiquarian book dealers would help by promoting the sharing of information. The ACRL's Library Security Committee has promulgated guidelines for what to do before, during, and after theft problems.

Model legislation for ensuring legal and law enforcement support is either on the books or pending in about 40 states, which have enacted measures in the last 10 years dealing with library theft and library violence. Libraries must form and join electronic networks of their own and talk to one another. Patterns may develop and lead to arrests. One problem with this form of communication, however, is that libraries do not really like to talk about their losses for fear of alienating the public, discouraging potential donors, and having to confess the embarrassing facts of lack of due diligence and vigilance.

Many security experts advocate, instead, concentric circles of security. The master plan is to impede and frustrate the suspect to the extent that he or she either becomes discouraged or makes a mistake. The concentric configuration should begin outside the building, and as the thief moves closer to the heart of the rare materials or other valuables collection, it becomes more difficult to penetrate the library's defences. Despite the predatory nature of some patrons, libraries should do all they can to keep materials available.

It is preferable to take one's losses while guaranteeing availability; others think that safety and security outweigh the desires and needs of patrons. Effective deterrents to theft and mutilation exist, but lack of funding may preclude their purchase and implementation. Even when funds are available, there is sometimes lack of commitment to security enforcement at administrative levels. Without the firm dedication of city, county, university officials, and library administrators, there is little chance for the library to do what is necessary to make it difficult for thieves and vandals to ply their trades. There is often a lack of awareness or indifference to the problem of library theft on the part of the criminal justice system, whose officers may feel they have more serious things to worry about.

SEXUAL BEHAVIOUR

Sexual behaviour ranging from blatant exhibitionism are interesting psychological problem, but they are undeniably a lot cheaper than going to a motel. The coast is usually clear because many libraries have no security force at all, while the security personnel of others are stretched thin, and are thus able to spend very little time observing human behaviour. There is usually a delicate and rather subjective line between what is actually criminal and what is merely offensive or in poor taste.

PREVENTION OF VIOLENCES

There are precautions that can be implemented that may serve to lessen the threat of violence. For example, the library could install metal detectors at all public entrances to the building. They were already part of the interior landscape of every airport, and while they may slow down the procedure of getting to one's plane, they are universally accepted now as the price of feeling more secure.

Libraries have no metal detectors at their doors; anyone is free to enter with anything they happen to be carrying concealed or in plain sight. But metal detectors are both expensive and labour-intensive in that they require personnel to spring into action when a weapon or other suspicious metallic object is detected. They are psychologically problematic in that some people resent the intrusion and the corresponding implication that they are not to be trusted. They are not foolproof. An umbrella, a cane, or even a library book, for example, may be employed as a lethal weapon, yet it is quite easy to enter a library with one, or, in the latter case, to find the place filled with them.

Rent Security

One preventive against unbridled misconduct is to hire security guards and charge them, among other duties, with examining the property of those entering and leaving the building. Sometimes security guards may require patrons to check their bags and other possessions in lockers; in others, they may be granted the right to search briefcases, book bags, and other luggage on demand.

Besides being a considerable expense, security guards tend to be more intent on finding books and other library property leaving the building illegally than they are on discovering concealed weapons being brought into the building, although both are important. Additionally, depending on local laws and ordinances, library employees may have no legal right to search the persons or belongings of their visitors, and insisting on doing so may leave the library legally vulnerable to lawsuits.

Restrict Access

Restricted access may be used to keep all unauthorised people out of some areas, or to prevent certain groups of people from entering off-limits parts of the building. While crime may occur anywhere on the premises or on the surrounding grounds, the largest proportion of library crime actually takes place in the non-public areas where perpetrators are not supposed to be.

Keeping the public out of unauthorised areas by making it impossible, or at least difficult, for them to enter will help reduce library crime. In some libraries, only borrowers who can produce and display valid and current borrower's cards are privileged to use the building. In other libraries, a current ID must be produced before the patron is granted admission to stack areas.

Security from Building Flaws

Libraries are usually easier places for criminal or deviant behaviour. Libraries are first of all deliberately free for all to enter. Many libraries are housed in old buildings with poor lighting. Many newer structures have been intentionally designed to provide charming, sequestered, out-of-the-way nooks and other places for quiet reading, contemplation, and study. Even if older buildings are renovated, aisles and alcoves are often secluded because people like them that way. There is limited constant hustle and bustle because people favour quiet in libraries, and quiet contributes to a place to concentrate undisturbed.

During early periods, most libraries were designed to house closed stacks, and were not intended for the public to browse; therefore, stack security was not much of an issue. Closed stacks, however, meant that staff members had to get items for patrons to take home or use in the reading rooms. The stacks did not have to be short enough to see over, around, or through, since they were intended for staff use only. Patrons had to submit call slips and wait for their books, while the stack areas were the province of speedy runners who were the only ones normally allowed into the book storage area. Gradually, due to changing times and changing user expectations, the stacks of almost all public and academic libraries were opened to the public. Thus they became ideal hangouts for thieves, thrill seekers, sexual cruisers, vandals, and others bent on mischief or mayhem.

In seeking to become more accessible to their users, libraries opened their stacks to browsers, which necessarily reduced the overall security level in favour of open access. The stacks have become great places to hide. Even unwarranted spying, surveillance, and monitoring of activity in the building may not actually overcome the ability of determined persons to commit violent acts. Even a library equipped with multiple surveillance cameras cannot expect to be able to monitor everyone's behaviour everywhere in the building at all times. Library design is another unfortunate factor in encouraging some types of problem patron behaviour. Some of the newest libraries feature recesses, alcoves, study carrels, and other remote spots where surveillance by staff is infrequent, unlikely, or just not possible, especially when the library is short-staffed.

Libraries attract potential criminals because they do not charge admission. Everyone is free to enter without challenge, interrogation, or proof of financial solvency. Nor can most libraries afford frequent security patrols—the cost of employing security guards is prohibitive for smaller libraries and difficult even for larger ones. Because library buildings are so accessible, in fact, they invite problems. They provide a free, safe haven for those who want to read or study or think, but they also cater to people who seek convenient places for their criminal behaviour.

Master Plan for Library Security

Those entrusted with protecting personal safety in libraries have differing opinions concerning the appropriate level of freedom that the public should enjoy. There are several points of almost total consensus, however. It is generally agreed by writers on building security for libraries that every library should perform as many of the following actions as possible in assessing and preserving its security posture:

i) Monitor crime patterns in the community, especially in the surrounding area of the library.

ii) Analyse the library's present security posture.

iii) Evaluate design flaws.

iv) Hire police or security guards.

v) Purchase security equipment or augment surveillance technology.

vi) Devise and implement a security checklist.

vii) Put a comprehensive security policy in place.

viii) Train all levels of staff in the elements of security and crisis management.

ix) Designate personnel as security monitors.

x) Screen future employees.

xi) Post behaviour policies in conspicuous places in more than one location.

xii) Have liability insurance coverage.

xiii) Network and maintain continual communication with other institutions who share your security risks and problems.

xiv) Do conspicuous monitoring.

Rules and Guidelines

No one in a library building is completely safe from attack by determined or demented individual's bent on doing mischief or harm to others. It is the librarian's professional nature to want to meet, interact with, and help patrons. Libraries cannot afford to be cavalier about public safety, figuring that patrons enter at their own risk. They must place the welfare of their visitors at the top of the list of imperatives. In today's society, library workers can find themselves subjected to public abuse, and they may even become the target of actual or threatened violence. In addressing this problem, many library ideals for providing aesthetically pleasing and easily accessible libraries may have to give way to more practical safety considerations.

Problematic people are as free to enter a library building as are considerate, normal people, every day and every evening. Libraries are often ideal outlets for their acting out their anger and other anti-social behaviours. Security patrols help, of course, but even libraries with uniformed security report failure to control behaviour everywhere in a large building.

Library design is another important factor in dealing with some types of problem patron behaviour. Libraries, because they do not charge admission, tend to attract all manner of weirdos and people bent on misbehaving. Most libraries cannot afford frequent security patrols, and thus provide a free, safe haven for those who seek places for their criminal or deviant behaviour. Guards and staff members entrusted with security, of course, work in existing buildings of finite size and dimensions, where responses to requests for revised architecture range anywhere from difficult to impossible.

The library should seek to adapt policies that are flexible but still meet consistent safety standards. In order to achieve this, however, the staff need to be clear on what behaviour they should and should not tolerate, and what to do when there clearly is a problem. Such lists should be in writing, circulated to all staff, and prominently posted in the library for the public to see. It is frequently very difficult to anticipate just what those consequences are going to be, especially when dealing with human behaviour. Working in a public place was easy, and part of the salary of every public employee compensates him or her for having, on occasion, to make difficult or distasteful choices regarding other people.

The cornerstone to dealing with problem patrons when they become difficult or dangerous is a strong and supportive administration that is willing to back up security measures with enforcement when necessary. In too many problem patron scenarios, nothing useful can be done by the staff because they have no support from the administration, who may fear adverse consequences if they give security staffers freedom of action.

If the library administration takes the same approach to problem patrons as ostriches are said to do to danger problems will continue and perhaps escalate. Both administration and staff need consensus on which behaviours are problematic, and decisions that will apply to everyone should be written into a security policy. Sometimes, however, just what is or is not a problem may be very difficult to codify and put in writing. Staff members and security personnel meeting and talking potential problems over before they become crises is one of the most effective forms of deterrence and is strongly recommended for all staff at all levels.

The best way to deal with a crisis is to prevent it from happening in the first place. Ten tips provided by US National Crisis Prevention Institute for crisis prevention are:

— Be empathic.
— Clarify messages.
— Respect personal space.
— Be aware of body position.
— Permit verbal venting where possible.
— Set and enforce reasonable limits.
— Avoid overreacting.

— Use physical techniques only as a last resort.

— Ignore challenge questions.

— Keep your non-verbal cues non-threatening.

The library should not tolerate any unauthorised person carrying firearms, deadly weapons, or clearly dangerous materials into the building or having them on the premises, in accordance with local laws. The library should attempt to detain and turn over to police authorities any visitors or staff members who violate criminal laws or who display a serious or immediate threat to themselves or others.

The library must not tolerate illegal, violent, abusive, or threatening behaviour, and each individual must be held accountable for his or her actions on library premises. Staff must require perpetrators to leave, even if the offence is not deemed serious or immediate enough to pose either a threat or a violation of local law.

Security or staff must intervene in each situation that is construed as an illegal act, that disrupts workers or facility operation, or that threatens to do so. Since the library needs to provide each visitor and staff member a safe facility, the governing agency must provide facilities, regulatory procedures, and inspections to promote safety and security. The library must therefore respond to each report of concern and seek to improve each questionable condition to everyone's satisfaction.

4
Ethical Issues

Before we attempt to discuss the legal and ethical aspects of human behaviour, let us distinguish as clearly as possible between legal matters and ethical matters in a library context. Where the law provides clearly for the illegality of certain acts, and provides for appropriate punishment for those committing the acts, we have a legal matter on our hands. Perhaps the most problematic area of difficulty for the library, however, lies in the shadowy realm of ethics, where there are no hard-and-fast rules, and where each person's conscience serves as the only guide. Ethical decision making, however, is all essay questions. One of the requirements of ethical decision making is original thought. Ethics is that process that makes you so uncomfortable that you can only escape from the situation by having to think.

There is a little larceny in each human soul which is only partly right. Experience teaches us that while there may be a little larceny in every soul, there is a lot of larceny in many more. And some of those souls, not surprisingly, focus their eyes on libraries and archival institutions. It may simply be human nature. Witness a recent survey in which high school seniors were asked if they would cheat on a test, falsify a report, misrepresent their income, and so on. While there are almost as many reasons for taking library materials without going through authorised procedures as there are actual cases of taking them, each instance is an ethical infraction both of the golden rule and library operating procedure.

Some library administrators have developed psychological tests that they administer to prospective employees, hoping to discover and weed out the bad apples, the larcenous, the incorrigible, the malevolent, the mentally unbalanced, and the downright sneaky. The jury is still out on the legality of such tests, however, and besides, it is unlikely that any diagnostic test will ever be devised to will distinguish trustworthy people from those less so. We may deplore or even deny the notion that everybody is a prospective or potential thief, but there it is, and we must deal with reality.

So since there seems to be no likelihood of perfecting humankind to the point that it refrains voluntarily from lying, cheating, stealing, or tolerating and covering up for, or enabling, those who do, enhanced and improved ongoing efforts in the direction of better library security are in order. Legal infractions, as contrasted with ethical lapses, are easily defined by consulting the state, local, or campus statutes concerning library property. And the really good thing about legal infractions is that they are spelled out carefully, and appropriate punishment is prescribed by law. It is, therefore, with ethical infractions that we need to be concerned, because such offences are subjectively defined and there is no consensus on how to respond to them.

THREATS TO PRIVACY

Privacy is the condition of being secluded or isolated from the view of, or from contact with others. In the age of the internet and other technological innovations that have found their way into common library use, such a set of definitions is woefully inadequate to the implications of the term. A better definition would include some notion of personal security as well, along with something about the right to be left alone. New thinkers, scholars, and practitioners are now considering privacy in the sense of the feeling a person has of being secure that personal and private transactions will remain personal and private unless he or she voluntarily chooses to share them with others.

The consensus among these thinkers is that privacy is not just an expected casualty of technology—it is already a victim, dead on arrival. Moreover, unless steps are taken immediately to ensure personal privacy, serious damage can and will be done to our personal freedoms, and to the way we feel about ourselves in regard to the freedom to do as we choose in this democracy. It is in this context that libraries must also consider the concept, because only when people like library users feel secure in their freedom from prying eyes and unwarranted interference will they maximise their use of libraries and other public utilities.

Without privacy, a chilling effect takes over, causing fearful and sensible persons to avoid inquiry into areas that might incur undesired scrutiny, and to fear the use of public channels such as the internet for their transactions, lest they be called upon to answer for what they want to know and why they want to know it.

Using ordinary library records the kind found in not just government or specialised files but in public libraries almost everywhere—one can, with internet access and a few hours of intensive work, assemble quite an impressive dossier about another person, consisting of, for example, that person's spending habits, medical history, financial holdings, and political affiliations. The information is out there, after all, and just waiting for someone to access it and draw inferences from it, fairly or unfairly. By applying such information, one can even assume the identity of another person, not in appearance, but enough to fool most computers into giving up even more secrets.

It is far too easy for criminals to perpetrate identity thefts in this way. It's really not all that hard to get a new driver's licence with your face stuck on the front and someone else's vital statistics typed next to the picture. Critics of state departments of motor vehicles say that the departments don't always question why someone is ordering a new driver's licence and having it sent to a new address. Retailers are supposed to ask for other pieces of identification before replacing a lost credit card but often do not.

Most people feel that when they signed up for a local library card, they were entering into a tacit contract with the library that their personal information would not be used in any way detrimental to them. But imagine the results if someone with access to the library's records decided to find out who was borrowing books on such topics as bomb-making, counter-espionage, AIDS treatment, or gay sex.

Just reading about a subject does not accuse anyone of anything, one's enemies or opponents could distort such facts into smoking guns of guilt and shame, and even cause law enforcement authorities to get interested in who's reading what. And with internet access to library records, there is even the possibility that those library records could be breached, replaced, defaced, or distorted until they contain potentially damaging or compromising information about you and your reading, listening, or viewing habits.

Privacy is not only a personal issue, but it is rapidly becoming a national priority as well. The US National Information Infrastructure is the result of a forum whose goal was to provide a mechanism for the library community to identify national policy issues, questions, and principles in the areas of telecommunications and information infrastructure.

Among the principles for the for the development of the US National Information Infrastructure, the following criteria are listed under the heading of privacy.

a) Privacy should be carefully protected and extended.
b) Comprehensive policies should be developed to ensure that the privacy of all people is protected.
c) Personal data collected to provide specific services should be limited to the minimum necessary.
d) Sharing data collected from individuals should only be permitted with their informed consent.
e) Individuals should have the right to inspect and correct data files about themselves.
f) Transaction data should remain confidential.

These principles are designed to protect the individual's right to be left alone while maximising public disclosure of public records. Naturally, the more barriers the library community finds it necessary to erect in the way of free and unfettered exchange of information, the more complicated and the slower transactional procedures will become. For example, detaining and interrogating visitors or surveillance of library areas is inimical to the notion of freedom. Moreover, they are labour-intensive and thus expensive practices, or more libraries would probably be doing them already.

Given library budgets, it is highly unlikely that library security will ever reach the level of airport security. Libraries are not hotbeds of criminal activity or places where people should be afraid to go or to spend time. But a prudent measure of building security seems indicated to ensure that they stay safe. Many methods of enhancing and maintaining security are low-cost, low-maintenance measures that the library can effect immediately.

Today the library will cease to exist as merely a large building containing books and other physical materials. For certain library users, that day has already arrived, in fact. For the rest of us, however, the date at which the library will exist only out there in cyberspace is still on its way. At that time, the chances of people being physically at risk in libraries should fall to zero, because they will not enter public buildings to accomplish their informational, educational, or recreational library needs. Everything will be available electronically, and it will be possible for citizens with access to appropriate technology to visit the library and make full use of its services without leaving home or even putting on their shoes. But such a brave new world scenario contains problems of its own if the future library is to be available to all citizens.

To begin with, accessing a library from home is impossible for unfortunates who have no homes. And what about people who have homes but lack computers, modems, or even telephones? Such persons would completely lack access to virtual libraries unless there is a public place where they are provided free access to systems and services. This solves the problem of the have-nots, perhaps, but gets us right back to libraries as public places, vulnerable to the ancient security concerns they have had all along.

A promising new technology deals with the electronic imaging of all documents in collections so that the original need never be displayed, and thus cannot be stolen, lost, or damaged, since the public deals only with cheap copies of inconsequential value. This would deal effectively with the problem of loss of valuable materials, reducing security concerns to the status of nuisances, rather than serious, costly losses.

INSIDE JOBS

Inside jobs, in which library employees misuse their positions to commit theft, are unfortunately ubiquitous, as library staff are in the most advantageous position to leave the building with our possessions. In a recent situation, theft was the issue at the Akron-Summit County (Ohio) Public Library and a security guard was the culprit. When police set up video surveillance inside the library to find out who was stealing videotapes and CDs, they caught the library guard, who was an employee of Ohio Security. Upon investigation, police found 72 videocassettes and seven compact discs valued at $1,363.21 in the guard's house and car. It would be very convenient if we could take on an us-versus-them position and consider all threats as coming from the public. But too often the greatest threat to our collections comes from those employed by the library.

In addition to inside jobs in which materials are purloined by staff members, there are numerous incidents involving threatening or criminal behaviour on the part of staff. It would be folly to pretend that they're not out there—those persons who would damage our libraries by theft, electronic mischief, or sheer negligence with cigarettes or food. What many librarians overlook or discount, however, is that such people aren't just out there. Inside jobs may be retributive or random, and may be premeditated or without any thought at all. Such acts may be drug or alcohol-induced or augmented, and the perpetrator may have a history of mental illness, depression, or addiction. A few may even be suicidal or beyond caring what they do or what happens to others.

Inside jobs are no doubt the most difficult acts to interdict or prevent because employees are normally spared the careful scrutiny accorded to members of the public in their visits to the building. Screening of all employees helps significantly, but a few staff members may have successfully concealed their addiction to narcotics and may need to steal to support their habits. What should the library do when it discovers that a staff member has been stealing? Guidelines may suggest what should be done, depending on the motive for the theft, what the rule book says, the personality of the administrator, and the importance to the library of the culprit. For first offences, where the motive is clearly not related to substance abuse, the range of penalties is considerable and can be any of the following, singly or in combination:

a) A stern warning and the requirement of a promise never to do it again.
b) A requirement that psychological counselling be sought immediately.
c) Being placed on probation for a specified time period.
d) Immediate transfer to a position that does not involve handling valuable items.
e) Demotion with reduction in salary.
f) Widespread publicity so that all staff and the outside world are made aware of the situation.
g) The summoning of police and the pressing of criminal charges.

We must acknowledge that many of our thefts are inside jobs carried out by library employees who often work with little supervision and who have access to expensive collections. There are ways to lessen the risk of such crimes. References on applications must be thoroughly checked. The use of a weighted application form produced by security consultants might be a start, but may be illegal in your area. There are inexpensive predictive tests available whose proponents claim can identify the potential for thievery, but many security experts challenge the effectiveness of such tests.

By ascribing a score to applicants' responses to certain test questions, security agents claim to be able to predict those more prone to steal, based on certain factors descriptive of those previously caught stealing. Recently, the American Psychological Association concluded that professionally developed integrity tests are valid predictors of dishonest and counterproductive behaviour in the workplace and are more scientifically acceptable than other predictors of theft.

The best way to keep workers from stealing is to refrain from hiring thieves in the first place. Better background checks would help a good deal. But many library managers prefer to trust their instincts in hiring, figuring that they are keen and perceptive judges of human nature. Hiring people by 'gut instincts' or 'chemistry' is too risky. It is too easy to make a mistake based only on appearances or what the applicant says about himself. Certain danger signs may point to crime-prone employees, or at least the ones to watch:

a) violation of company policies on a regular basis
b) record of frequent tardiness or absenteeism
c) display of a poor attitude, erratic behaviour, or constant complaints
d) frequent patron complaints about the employee
e) unexplained shrinkage of materials or supplies inventory
f) products found concealed in areas accessible only to employees
g) discrepancies in accounts
h) unexplained losses from petty cash.

Every library should dedicate itself to following such basic steps as the following:

a) Investigate all applicants by means of pre-employment background checks.
b) Be suspicious. Do not rely on what prospective employees tell you about themselves.
c) A clearly written policy covering appropriate staff conduct in dealing with the public—including both verbal and physical harassment or intimidation—should be circulated to all employees for their signatures.
d) The library should attempt to create as humane a termination policy as possible to lessen negative feelings among those fired.

e) Tighten security by posting loss-prevention rules in conspicuous places.
f) Verify petty cash totals daily and lock the safe at night.
g) Consider random drug testing of all staff.
h) Conduct workshops and discussions on dishonesty and consequences.
i) Enforce strict lock and key access.
j) Promulgate a system-wide honour system. The honour system frequently does not prevent larceny, but it is always worth a try, especially when those found to be in breach of the code know that they will be summarily fired.
k) Prosecute staff members who commit crimes.
l) One persistent problem among staff members is the emotional disinclination to tell on a fellow employee, colleague, or friend. Whistle-blowing, while not universally applauded, should be encouraged so that staff feel willing to report theft, substance abuse, or emotional instability. Employees should be encouraged to report any suspicious activity immediately. They should also be encouraged to overcome their fear of making a mistake or getting involved.

When employees log on to corporate computer systems, they get a stern reminder that the data they are accessing are confidential and proprietary, and that misuse or malfeasance could get them fired and possibly prosecuted. Libraries, too, are moving to protect themselves similarly from their own employees. Much attention has been given to outside hackers who electronically break into sensitive computer files, but many administrators will attest that dishonest and incompetent employees do the most damage.

Libraries are not normally in possession of competitive or proprietary information. However, more and more libraries are writing and enforcing strict policies for computer use by employees, sometimes even installing expensive electronic gear to detect violations. Violators are often fired. But employees and security consultants acknowledge that just having a policy helps keep people honest. Some enforcement measures may come close to invading worker privacy. It is impossible to tell just how big a problem computer abuse is for two reasons. First, victims of computer abuse are rarely willing to talk about it for fear of looking stupid or careless. Second, it is in the nature of computer abuse that the victims are not always aware their materials have been stolen until long after the event.

Less than two per cent of incidents of employee theft are reported to authorities, according to a survey by the Data Processing Management Association. Employee abuse, including fraud, software copyright infringement, and loss or theft of information, clearly costs companies and libraries hundreds of millions of dollars a year. Whom to trust with sensitive information and data is among a manager's worst nightmares. There is no sure way to guarantee that employees will be honest and ethical, despite all manner of psychological tests.

A library contracts with a major commercial online database supplier for unlimited searches for an annual fee. This means that anyone in possession of a user identification and current password can search hundreds of online databases free and do as they like with the information. It is one of the unique properties of information that one can give it away limitless times and still have it. This is at once the best and worst feature of information, and the one that proves the trickiest for libraries to control.

The true value of a policy that expressly lists prohibitions is that it helps make penalties stick. It is important to impress all employees with computer access that breaking into other people's files and personal records is improper behaviour. With a policy in force, the library has a strong basis for taking action against offenders. Another way to enforce the policy is to require all new employees to sign forms saying that they have read the library's computer and confidentiality policies and agree to abide by their terms.

One major problem with purchasing sophisticated monitoring systems is that the capability of employers to monitor who is using computers and what is being entered into them looks like 'big brotherism'. Many staff find such monitoring unwarranted, an unpleasant intrusion into their privacy, and a tacit statement that library managers trust no one to behave responsibly and ethically. Another problem is 'Who's going to watch the watchers?' This is only an admission that, human nature being what it is, no one is above suspicion, and managers are as likely to be transgressors as line staff. Unauthorised telephone calls are another problem. Forcing employees to pay for calls not related to the library's business seems only appropriate; firing those so apprehended may seem extreme. Yet making personal calls on company time and over company lines is another form of theft and should be dealt with in the same way as the library deals with those who steal books or mutilate magazines.

Libraries must accept a certain amount of unauthorised use of its resources but may conclude that overt prosecution of those who are caught may be counterproductive. Smarter and happier people work in places that allow them to be innovative, which may mean looser rules. Violating the privacy of others with computers, however, is a serious matter, and should be dealt with seriously. Employers expect and need honest, trustworthy employees. There is also the very real threat of lawsuits, as libraries are vulnerable to suit by injured patrons. Screening services are available, and they are good at finding things out about potential employees.

5

Information Control

In any organisation there is data which is sensitive or valuable or both. It is impossible to achieve total security over machine-processed data, but effective security and control procedures can considerably reduce the risks of misuse or disclosure of data. Increasing complexity of the controls needed to guard against these risks has led to the development of expertise in data security within the data processing, consulting and audit communities. Knowledge and techniques are developed through academic study, industrial research and practical experience, and are in turn disseminated through courses, conferences, articles and textbooks. The majority of data processing users are now aware of at least some of the threats to the integrity of their data.

No matter how good the protective measures, there will always be some means of damaging the computer or data. The objective of any review of security is to minimise the exposure that a company faces. There are a large number of techniques available to enhance security and not all will be useful or applicable in any particular organisation. The level of expenditure on protection needs to be related to the degree of vulnerability of the computer system and the value of the data in question. If the effects of loss or damage would be extremely expensive to a company it is clearly worth substantial expenditure to prevent them from occurring. If other data were lost or incorrect the effects might be inconvenient but not disastrous and the precautions should not therefore be so elaborate.

can demand to see student or other identification, with the assumptive right to eject persons who do not produce valid reasons for being there. Public library patrons, however, are not required to belong to anything, or even to reside in the jurisdictional area of the library, giving the guards much less latitude as to what they can ask and of whom.

Courtroom trials take time and money. Money is entailed when the library must hire legal representation to defend itself against harassment suits. And do not forget the dollars in lost employee time while they appear in court. In short, we have to be willing to go all the way with our charges or they become meaningless, and the library will have lost, in addition to time and money, the threat of deterrence.

5

Information Control

In any organisation there is data which is sensitive or valuable or both. It is impossible to achieve total security over machine-processed data, but effective security and control procedures can considerably reduce the risks of misuse or disclosure of data. Increasing complexity of the controls needed to guard against these risks has led to the development of expertise in data security within the data processing, consulting and audit communities. Knowledge and techniques are developed through academic study, industrial research and practical experience, and are in turn disseminated through courses, conferences, articles and textbooks. The majority of data processing users are now aware of at least some of the threats to the integrity of their data.

No matter how good the protective measures, there will always be some means of damaging the computer or data. The objective of any review of security is to minimise the exposure that a company faces. There are a large number of techniques available to enhance security and not all will be useful or applicable in any particular organisation. The level of expenditure on protection needs to be related to the degree of vulnerability of the computer system and the value of the data in question. If the effects of loss or damage would be extremely expensive to a company it is clearly worth substantial expenditure to prevent them from occurring. If other data were lost or incorrect the effects might be inconvenient but not disastrous and the precautions should not therefore be so elaborate.

The vulnerability to a certain event can be defined as the cost that an organisation would incur if the event took place. The likelihood of these occurrences also needs to be considered and various precautions can be taken to reduce the probability of, for example, a fire or loss by embezzlement. Exposure to a certain event can be defined as the vulnerability to that event multiplied by the probability of its occurrence within a given time. The overall exposure of an organisation to its data processing facility is the sum of the exposures for the various individual events that could occur.

A security programme must be designed to protect an installation both from major disasters that occur rarely, such as fires and large embezzlements, and from smaller events such as operator error which can occur several times each week. To reduce the exposure, the security programme must use the following methods.

i) *Minimise the probability of a breach happening.* An important part of any security programme is prevention and this can apply both to physical security and discouraging manipulation and embezzlement.

ii) *Identify that a problem has occurred.* The security of the installation and the controls surrounding the systems should provide details which will reveal that an unauthorised event happened. These details should be produced regularly and reviewed at reasonable intervals.

iii) *Minimise the damage of an event.* Once a fire has started or a file place should be sufficient to isolate the event and restrict the effects to a small area.

iv) *Design a method of recovering from the damage.* It is important for the continuity of the business that recovery is both quick and effective, whether it requires the replacement of equipment or reconstruction of a file.

There are a number of fundamental points which can be used in marketing a data security review. These topics are wide ranging and will be understandable to both senior management as well as to their data processing management.

The spread of computer use during the last century has brought a whole new set of problems with security implications, many of which we are only now beginning fully to appreciate. Hard facts about computer-linked crime are notoriously difficult to come by. This is understandable where commerce and industry are concerned, since no one finds it easy to admit to mistakes, nor to risk the evaporation of business confidence that might all too readily follow a public admission of corporate loss. An open examination of those criminal actions taken against computer systems would lead to more effective precautions and counteractions.

The possibility of greater publicity attending computer crimes in the future has not been helped by the way in which public attitudes have been conditioned by the media to regard all such activity as amorous 'high-tech' crime, and the perpetrators as 'whizz kids'. Today there is a very equivocal attitude to the morality of any activity involving computer abuse.

Mike Comer, an expert investigator of computer fraud, recently stated that his current portfolio of cases carried a value worldwide of $150 million, of which only 10 per cent by value had been reported to the police. Nor is it the view of the British police that the problem is an insignificant one. Computer-linked crime will become one of the major criminal activities of the next decade, and argue that the rapid spread of computer literacy in our society will not be confined merely to the honest citizen. Computer skills will inevitably be misused. They potentially offer far richer and easier pickings for the criminal than armed robbery.

An analysis of those 67 crimes reported by the Audit Inspectorate in 1981 in US reveals the following pattern:

a) Input manipulation: 42 cases
b) Output manipulation: 2 cases

c) Programme alteration: 1 cases
d) Resource misuse: 22 cases.

Majority of abuses are manipulation of input or misuse of computer resources, though we should be careful of placing too much weight on what is only a small sample. The analysis makes sense, in that the ability to commit a crime by manipulating input data requires a lower level of computing skills than does altering a programme; whilst the opportunity data into the computer system, and is not restricted to the computer specialists. This problem serves to illustrate two of the ways in which developments in the technology of computing have brought additional difficulties to controlling fraud. One is the problem of preserving written records of transactions in these days of interactive computing, where there is the ready facility to make direct alterations of the computer-held records. The other concerns the difficulties of maintaining the separation of duties between those responsible for the physical handling and control of goods or services and those whose job it is to record such transactions. In the search for alternative controls, increased reliance has been placed on the computer system's specification and the programming. For this reason, the documentation of the systems and programmes has become vitally important in the defence against fraud. The concept of the separation of duties has moved inside the computer department, where it implies the need to keep functionally and physically separate the work of analysts, programmers, operators and data entry staff.

A simple illustration of what can happen if this basic concept is ignored occurred a few years ago in a computer bureau. A clerk prepared payroll input sheets and submitted the list for authorisation. It was signed, but not totalled, and returned to the clerk for processing. The clerk then added some extra amounts, knowing that the list would not be checked again. With the benefit of hindsight, it is quite easy to see what was wrong in the situation just described. However, that clerk's position accurately reflected what happens in offices up and down the country. Inevitably, we could not operate in our commercial lives without trusting people, but it remains a fact that where the opportunity, technical ability, and the means of converting fraudulent actions to cash coincide, then there is great scope for crime.

There are four kinds of computer security threats: interruption, interception, modification and fabrication.

i) *Interruptions*: These include any delay or disruption of normal business operations. Computer down time caused by viruses and their removal is a very common problem today.

ii) *Interceptions*: These are unauthorised access to information, which may or may not result in the illicit use of data. Browsing through stored files and monitoring network or telephone transfers are considered access. There are hundreds of methods to remotely gain unauthorised access to computer systems over a network.

iii) *Modification*: Modification includes tampering with information once access has been achieved by changing software or hardware controls or the data itself. Think of the consequences if an intruder changed the amounts owed to your company by outside vendors.

iv) *Fabrication*: It means fraud and counterfeiting. It is modification in a way to benefit the intruder or to cause problems for the corporation. It can involve skilfully adding data or objects to the computing system such as transactions or additional files on a database.

A typical data security programme should involve both people and information. The activities should included in such a programme are:

i) Prevention

ii) Protection

iii) Detection/investigation

iv) Damage assessment

v) Recovery.

Policies are the high level guidance or vision directing the organisation. The statement establishes the basic philosophy of the organisation and determines the functional areas where controls must be established. Implemented by management to provide information, control and direction, the IS security policy is used to support the development of the subsequent security programme.

A good infosecurity programme policy statement must do a number of things:

i) Identify information assets.

ii) Define who is responsible for classifying and valuing information assets and who must comply.

iii) Describe the role of employees in protecting information.

iv) Provide for monitoring and enforcement.

The security policy statement should describe what information should be protected as well as the extent of allowable distribution. Responsibilities should address all levels of the organisational structure, stating who is responsible for complying with the policy and who is responsible for making sure that the classifying policies are enforced. Monitoring and enforcement address when the policy becomes effective, conditions under which the policy is enforced, and how it will be monitored.

The policy statement must also be unambiguous, so that no one can be exempted from the requirements. One method of ensuring accountability is to incorporate an employee acceptance page at the end of the document which must be signed and returned to appropriate management personnel.

To protect people as well as data, the following guidelines should be implemented:

i) Guard against and remove from unnecessary temptation inappropriate data that employees might be exposed to while fulfilling job responsibilities.

ii) Ensure management awareness of the need for security, and their participation in the development and implementation of security policies.

iii) Insure the protection of sensitive or confidential data.

iv) Provide protection from acts that would cause malfunctions, errors and omissions, inaccuracy, unauthorised disclosure or destruction of data.

v) Insure the controls and procedures are in place that allow immediate detection and countermeasure implementation for information threats.

vi) Protect management from charges of imprudence in the event of information compromise.

vii) Insure the ability of the organisation to survive business interruptions and function adequately afterwards.

Proper data security is not solely the result of effective day-to-day procedures within the data processing department. The importance should be reflected in strategic plans and routine procedures. The background of the company organisation should be reviewed to identify any potential sources of increased security risk. The attitude of the client towards data processing and the presence of a computer strategy, integrated with the corporate plan, will have a significant effect on data security.

Analysis of the organisation structure enables us to evaluate the security practices and procedures in place and the role of the officers responsible for them. There should be someone who is responsible for security, even if it is by default. The job definition of that person should be reviewed to ensure that it is comprehensive and complete, and the results of their work should be examined for effectiveness.

Employees are simultaneously a company's principal security threat and the first line of defence in a security programme. The personnel-related topics are fundamental to the whole area of data security review. Personnel policies are important in order to ensure that all staff are aware of their responsibilities and that precautions are taken to protect the organisation from excessive dependence on important individuals. The policies and procedures followed when a person is recruited or leaves the organisation should always include an awareness of the security risks of these actions.

References must always be taken up for new recruits. People leaving the company should be moved to a non-sensitive role or asked to depart immediately after resigning. The internal audit department may act as a data security control and review body depending on their structure, staffing, training and charter. The internal audit staff should include people of sufficient expertise and training to enable them to review an installation or system in detail. The scope of their work should be wide enough to include all areas of potential risk, and they should have sufficient influence and status for their findings and recommendations to be accepted and implemented. The maintenance agreements should be regularly reviewed and renewed to ensure that all the computer equipment and ancillary equipment are covered.

An effective security programme must be well balanced among these various aspects. Too often, management has concentrated its efforts in one area leaving gaping holes elsewhere. Security can be categorised as follows:

i) *Physical security:* Physical security is concerned with safeguarding the hardware used during the processing of data and the media on which the data reside. Physical security includes protection against fire, flood, explosion, malicious destruction, and the provision of contingency planning arrangements to take effect in the event of a catastrophic occurrence at the main computer facility.

ii) *Employee education:* An aware employee educated to the needs of system security and privacy safeguards is perhaps the strongest control against many of the causes of exposure relating to data security. The employee must also be made aware of the disciplinary action which will be taken against anyone who violates company guidelines in this area.

iii) *Logical security:* Logical security refers to the software or hardware-wired controls built into the system to prevent or detect unauthorised entry into the system or unauthorised access to system or business data. Logical controls include the use of passwords to gain entry into the system and cryptography techniques which ensure that sensitive data are only available in clear text mode to authorised programmes which process those data.

There are several categories of controls, within each of the categories of security, which can be implemented to act upon a particular cause of exposure. It is imperative to take a balanced approach toward the introduction of controls. It would be courting disaster, not to mention the height of arrogance, to rely solely on preventive controls without providing adequate detective and/or corrective controls. The various categories of controls are as follows:

i) *Deterrent*: These controls are designed to deter people from trying to penetrate the security system. An example of this type of control is a management policy statement clearly defining what will happen to anyone caught violating security measures.

ii) *Preventive*: These controls prevent the cause of exposure from occurring at all or at least minimise the possibility; for example, password control at the terminal level in an online system will prevent unauthorised access to the system.

iii) *Detective*: Where an exposure has occurred, detective controls will report its existence in an effort to minimise the extent of the damage. Certain fire precautions fall into this category.

iv) *Corrective*: These controls are necessary to recover from a loss situation. Without corrective controls a company may go out of business because of inability to recover essential data after a catastrophe.

Physical Security

Physical security is the controls within the data centre, designed to safeguard the hardware used during the processing of the data and the media on which the data reside. It also involves the administrative controls that ensure a smooth and secure interface between people and the computer. The budget to make provisions for security will undoubtedly be limited so it must be used effectively. The installation of closed-circuit TV and complex mantraps will be meaningless if proper control is not maintained over the creation of back-up files or if the administrative procedures for the handling and distribution of sensitive reports are inadequate.

The measures of physical security are the most visible, and there may be a tendency to concentrate on the more glamorous of these measures to the exclusion of less ostentatious but equally effective ones. A balanced approach to the introduction of physical security measures will ensure that the budget is applied for maximum coverage.

It is necessary for the company to address the following specific tasks:

i) Evaluate the physical threats to the data-centre and determine the probability of occurrence for each threat.
ii) Estimate the potential losses to which the data centre is exposed in the event of an occurrence of one of the causes of exposure previously identified. The objective of calculating the potential loss estimate is to identify critical aspects of the data centre operation.

iii) Determine the annual loss expectancy by combining the estimates of the value of potential loss and probability of loss.

iv) When the estimate of annual loss has been completed, management will have a clear picture of the significant threats and will be able to assess the relevancy of various security measures in relation to their cost and their effect on the significant threats.

Duties' segregation

Segregation of duties ensures that one person cannot initiate, authorise, and process a transaction and have sole possession of the output from that transaction. It is often overlooked when a computer system is introduced. It was effectively implemented by placing specific responsibilities in distinct departments within the company. Accountants and auditors have built up a great deal of experience and expertise in the area of segregation of duties within manual systems.

Within a computerised environment the functions which were previously split between several departments may now be centralised within the data centre. Although the responsibility for the initiation and authorisation of transactions should remain within the originating department, the recording of these transactions onto computer-readable media will be the responsibility of the data centre. In some instances the computer programmes designed to process these transactions will authorise them based on certain predetermined conditions; for example, if a check drawn on an account will overdraw the account, the system may authorise payment based on an overdraft limit maintained for that account.

Adequate segregation of duties must exist within the data processing department and that this segregation must include the interface between the data processing department and the user groups. The data centre has custodial responsibility for all data held on computer-readable media.

The physical security measures are, therefore, the responsibility of the data centre. Responsibility for the integrity of the data maintained on computer media, however, remains with the appropriate user or technical department. Although the controls to protect the integrity of this data may be designed and implemented by the system designers and programmers responsible for the system, ultimately the user department is still responsible for the integrity of its business data. Changes to production libraries should be physically effected by one of the groups within the data centre. The initiation, authorisation, and actual change will be the responsibility of an applications group with the approval of the appropriate user department.

Access control

Access control provides the ability to grant selective access to certain people at certain times and deny access to all others at all times. The client will normally have addressed the question of restricting access to the computer area. We should also ensure that the controls are applied to all vulnerable and sensitive areas and that all staff and visitors are monitored.

There are a wide range of access control devices and techniques and the applicability of these will vary from site to site depending on the facility itself, the data processed and the cost involved. The computer facilities and their uninterrupted use can be affected by hazards of both man-made and natural origin. The possibility of these events should be recognised and measures taken to prevent or avoid them. Arrangements should be made to contain the hazard and to minimise the effects should it occur. The most common type of hazards affecting computers are fire and flood, occurring either within the computer area itself or outside, but with an impact upon data processing. Some locations are also liable to more exotic hazards such as tornadoes, earthquakes and lightning.

Before deciding on controlled access devices, the data centre management must assess exactly what they are trying to protect. Keeping non-personnel out of the building is fine, as far as it goes, but if personnel have the run of the building once inside the main door, then the overall security of the data centre is minimal. Once the data centre management has assessed which areas should be considered as sensitive, only those employees whose work routine requires access on a daily basis should be allowed unrestrained access. An important part of any controlled access system concerns the administrative procedures which give direction on allowing access, on a controlled basis, to anyone who has a legitimate cause to be in a restricted area.

Security of telecommunications

Almost 90 per cent of all data processing installations utilise some form of transaction processing based on telecommunications networks. From an audit point of view the use of telecommunications networks is a double-edged sword, in that it can be used to effectively control access to computing facilities but it can also lead to potential security problems, particularly with the increased number of entry points to the computing facilities and therefore to the computer data files. Computer security is no longer a question of ensuring that unauthorised persons cannot enter the computer room by installing card-key systems, etc., but of ensuring that, when a request is made to access the computer from perhaps hundreds of miles away, the correct person is allowed to access the network, and that they only access facilities which they have been authorised to access.

Extensive use of telecommunications networks has also raised unique problems in the area of restart and recovery, particularly where users of the remote facility have become more and more dependent on the use of the central facilities.

In reviewing a telecommunications network it is convenient to break the task into four distinct areas:

i) Network control function, including responsibilities for control over the elements in the teleprocessing network, and ensuring that the segregation of duties is adequate.

ii) Physical security of the equipment and lines used in the network.

iii) Logical access controls over the applications and systems that run on the network.

iv) Backup and recovery routines to ensure the continuity and reliability of the network.

Security of office systems

The sharing of data between many users and several application systems creates a need for a central responsible authority with the ability to control the structure and content of the database, the integrity of data within it and the limitation of access to it. This is the role of the database administrator. All systems requiring access to the database should use a common definition of each element in the database and should apply standard edit and validation tests for updating the database.

A new area of security risk arises in relation to word processors, microcomputers, and other office systems, with the spread of computing power into the user departments and away from the central data processing function.

The overriding risk to microcomputers results from the equipment itself. Due to the size and weight of a microcomputer it is very portable and is therefore prone to theft. This danger applies equally to components of the equipment, especially the printed circuit boards, which could be used in identical or compatible units.

The distribution of computing power will also provide the facility to input and process data using packaged software or application programmes which are developed in-house, but not by trained programmers. The use of these programmes to process financial data or to process information which is used to make important management decisions is an area of concern. The quality and integrity of the programme must be sufficiently high for the client to rely upon the output.

The installation of a microcomputer will need to be reviewed for the same areas as a mainframe, but the extent and depth of the review will need to be modified in light of the particular installation. Data security is the standards and procedures that protect data against unauthorised disclosure, modification or destruction, whether accidental or intentional. Within a computer environment, it is convenient to categorise data into two types:

i) *Business data*: It comprises all the computer-held information maintained by the various application programmes in support of the business requirements of the company.

ii) *System data*: It comprise the vendor-supplied operating system, utility programmes, compilers, and the application programmes developed or to meet the business requirements of the company.

Environmental safeguards

Fire precautions: Fire precautions can be considered in the categories of those that prevent the fire from occurring, those that detect the fire's occurrence or the imminence of a fire, and those that endeavour to correct the situation with the minimum of damage. Within each of these categories the controls can be further broken down into those that are people dependent and those that are mechanical.

The preventive controls include:

i) The materials used in the construction of the data centre should have an adequate fire rating.

ii) The design of the building should minimise the possibility of fire spreading from one area to another.

iii) Administrative procedures should be designed and implemented to avoid the risk of fire.

The detective controls include:

i) Detective controls should be designed to detect the early signs of a fire, activate the corrective device, and provide an audible warning to employees of the danger.

ii) Heat detectors, smoke detectors, and manually activated fire alarms should be placed in strategic areas within the data centre.

iii) Administrative procedures should describe the people-dependent functions to be activated in the event of fire.

The corrective controls include:

i) Water is still widely used as an extinguishing agent for fire and can be applied at the scene of the fire by means of a sprinkler system activated by the detection controls mentioned previously. The advantage of using water in fire fighting is its low cost relative to other means.

ii) Halon and carbon dioxide are gases used in fire fighting especially where electrical equipment may be involved. The use of carbon dioxide must be carefully controlled and the area evacuated before its use because of its harmful effects on people.

iii) Personnel should be trained in what they are to do in the event of fire.

iv) Fire marshals should be appointed for each department or functional area with specific responsibilities for their area.

v) Emergency exits and all fire-fighting equipment should be clearly sign-posted.

vi) The fire department should be invited to review the fire precautions within the data centre. Since the fire department maybe called into fight afire, it would be advantageous if they were aware of the layout of the data centre and what fire righting facilities were readily available and their location.

vii) After the fire has been brought under control and extinguished, there should be clearly defined procedures for getting the data centre back into production status.

Housekeeping habits: Some important reasons for good housekeeping habits are given below:

i) Large amounts of paper stored in the computer room can create a fire hazard; allowing operators to smoke while working is another potential source of fire.

ii) Food and drink should not be allowed into the computer room. A drink spilled down the back of the CPU is virtually guaranteed to cause a system failure.

iii) Inadequate filing of tapes and disks can cause operational problems and a security exposure. If files are continually misplaced, it may take a long time to realise that a file has been stolen.

iv) Management tolerance of poor housekeeping habits is not conducive to establishing the level of awareness about security desirable among employees in a computer environment.

Insurance: Insurance should be taken out as a conscious effort to cover exposures which cannot be totally eliminated by other means and whose cost of occurrence would be too high to absorb. Many types of insurance policies are available, each with its own limitations and endorsements. Generally speaking, the wider the coverage, the greater the cost. The premiums payable or indeed the availability of insurance will depend on the other components of the programme.

Some high-level descriptions of the types of policies are listed below.

i) Policies to cover physical damage or destruction of the hardware and media.

ii) Policies to cover the cost of recreating data are available at additional cost. Adequate backup procedures, including the use of off-site storage, can reduce the need for a policy of this type.

iii) Policies to cover the loss of business due to an insured peril. A company may suffer from severe competitive disadvantage if its data centre is put out of action for an extended period of time owing to afire.

Contingency plans

Contingency planning requires a commitment on the part of senior company management and not just data processing management. It concerns establishing procedures and facilities to counteract a prolonged failure or unavailability of hardware, software, or telecommunications. The increased use of computers has resulted, in many cases, in a reliance to the point where the company would cease to function if the computer facilities were unavailable for any length of time. The number of computer users who do not give serious thought to contingency planning or who go no farther than the thinking stages is astonishing. Effective contingency plans can range from establishing a second site with comparable facilities to the main processing centre, to establishing procedures for returning to the manual system that was in place before the introduction of the computer system. The extent of the alternate arrangements depends upon the degree to which the company relies upon the computer and the size, complexity, and criticality or the applications run on the computer.

The specific tasks which should be addressed include:

i) *Threat analysis:* Evaluate the threats to the data centre and determine the probability of occurrence for each threat and the estimated time to recover from such an occurrence.

ii) *Loss potential analysis:* Estimate the potential losses to which the data centre is exposed. The objective is to identify critical aspects of the data centre operation and to place a dollar value on the loss estimate.

iii) *Annual loss expectancy:* Combine the estimates of the value of potential loss and probability of loss to develop an estimate of annual loss expectancy. The purpose of this exercise is to pinpoint the significant threats as a guide to the selection of contingency arrangements. The cost of contingency arrangements should relate to the loss against which they provide protection.

iv) *Remedial measures:* When the estimate of annual loss has been completed, management will have a clear picture of the significant threats and critical applications. It will then be necessary to evaluate the recovery plans already in place to counter short-term failures and determine what additional measures, if any, are required to provide a cost-effective, secure environment which can handle both short and long-term failure or unavailability of hardware, software, or telecommunications.

Physical security of data is the most basic form of data processing control and is the area most commonly addressed, with greater or lesser effectiveness.

Security of programmes of data in this modern environment is dependent on effective password controls. These may be limited to simple sign-on passwords for terminal users, but can extend to definitions of individual access rights to programme functions, libraries and data files. The principal areas to be examined are:

i) user identification;
ii) data file protection; and
iii) programme security.

User identification covers the need for the user to identify himself to the system and for that identity to be authenticated. Following this the system may check whether the user has been given the authorisation to perform certain actions such as input, delete and update on certain data using specified programmes. Thus the system must perform a check for each connection of a user to a programme or data. Inappropriate or unauthorised attempts should be prevented and the attempts reported. A log should be automatically kept both in security purposes and to provide an audit trail, which should regularly reviewed. This security system should apply to all use data and programmes and operate continuously for every terminal.

User identification includes the control of password allocation of definition, the method of distributing the passwords, and the frequency of updating passwords. The role of the security officer is encompass some of these activities, including the definition a distribution of passwords. The reviewer should consider whether the controls examined also apply to the execution of batch jobs.

Some systems do not provide continuing security so that, for example, parts of a backup tape can be accessed by any user if the tape itself available. Data files and programme libraries may be protected by operation software password controls or by a software security package. The protection may exist only at file or library level, but in certain circumstances and environments it may apply at data element library member level. The security of datafiles becomes irrelevant if there is inadequate control over access to production programmes.

Integrity of the operating system software is fundamental to security of data processing. Although this area is notoriously difficult to review and to control effectively because of the wide-range capabilities and access rights of systems programmers, certain bad controls can be introduced to protect the system software from unauthorised manipulation or accidental damage.

It is important to ensure that only authorised versions of the system software are used and that any changes made are proper controlled. The minimum number of people should have the expert and facility to make amendments to system software. A record should be kept showing the details of the software so that a changes made can be identified, including the reason and the person responsible. This record should be reviewed regularly by processing management.

In a similar way the utility programmes within the system should be used to make modifications to data, programmes or system software without control and appropriate authorisation, and without leaving an audit trail. Powerful utilities should be closely controlled and could be kept off-line to improve security.

Controls over operations are examined under the following headings:

i) Scheduling and monitoring.
ii) Daily operations.
iii) Production programmes.
iv) Media control.

In order to ensure that authorised jobs, and only authorised jobs, are run against production data, it is important that production jobs are run in a planned and predictable sequence. This requires the preparation of a schedule by an authorised person, and the comparison of this schedule with the log of actual jobs run to ensure that complete processing has occurred and to prevent the use of unauthorised jobs. The use of cataloguing or macros should be encouraged because this automates, to a large extent, the running of jobs. This removes the need for operator intervention and reduces the possibility of an error being made or an incorrect instruction being submitted.

Programme security is again examined in this sub-section. Where there is a direct overlap with questions already asked concerning logical access, it is often a good idea to re-examine the security of production programmes from the operations viewpoint. In addition to preventing the processing of unauthorised jobs, operations procedures should ensure the use of correct datafiles. This can be achieved by controlling the issue and use of media and by the programmes themselves checking file labels and run-to-run totals.

Application programmes should always check that the correct file has been mounted and that the latest version is used. Many organisations are becoming almost totally dependent on their data processing systems for basic business and accounting support. The ability to recover from problems ranging from a system failure through to the complete destruction of the installation is therefore of critical importance.

By adopting good operating and programming techniques a programme can be restarted and processing can continue. A serious problem may result in the loss or corruption of data. Then the availability of backup data will allow processing to be restarted from a known and predictable point. This can only happen if a routine is established and followed to provide regular copies of valuable data which are securely stored and readily available. A partial or complete loss of the computing facility will cause the organisation to invoke a disaster plan of greater or lesser effectiveness. This usually involves moving the operation to an alternative site.

Whether data are maintained in filing cabinets within each department or in an integrated data base covering all aspects of the company's operation, it is desirable to protect such data against unauthorised disclosure, modification, or destruction.

Computerisation has centralised the maintenance of data previously distributed throughout the many departments of the company and allowed extremely fast and efficient access to these data. The exposures relating to computer-held data are the same as those relating to manually or electromechanically maintained data, but the magnitude of the exposure has increased greatly. This aspect is particularly relevant in the light of the current trend toward the database environment and the resultant significant increase in opportunities for the unauthorised modification, disclosure, or destruction of sensitive data.

Another significant trend at the present time is toward the use of minicomputers both as stand-alone systems and as components in a distributed processing network. The proliferation in the use of stand-alone minicomputers is attributable to the significant reduction in price due to recent technological advances which have brought minicomputers within the reach of smaller businesses and the continuing awareness by businessmen of the advantages of computerisation.

Logical Security

The term 'logical security' refers to the software or hardware-wired controls built into the system to prevent or detect unauthorised entry into the system.

Vendor controls

Vendor controls ensures that data are not lost or amended during transmission from the media into main storage.

Parity-bit checking: Parity-bit checking entails adding one bit to each character processed. Computers are built to accept either even or odd parity. The parity bit is added to ensure that the count of 'on' bits is odd or even depending on the type of computer. When the computer accepts odd parity, the count of all 'on' bits within a character must be an odd number.

File labels: Vendor-supplied software will generally attach header and trailer labels to data files created. The header labels can be used to determine that the correct file is being used and can also protect the file from being over-written before a specified date. Trailer labels can contain the number of blocks written into the file. This block count can then be checked after the file has been read to ensure that all the blocks have been read and that additional data have not been inserted.

Cryptography

The recent trend in database environment has caused a significant increase in opportunities for the unauthorised access to or disclosure of sensitive information. More and more applications are being designed as real-time, online systems, with the result that an increasing amount of confidential or sensitive data is being transmitted over telecommunication lines. Encryption techniques are designed to scramble the data into a form which is unintelligible to the unauthorised observer. Decryption techniques are then used to translate this scrambled text back into its original form. The advantages of encryption are that the encrypted data are secure from unauthorised disclosure or amendment, including the addition of any information. The introduction of the computer has enabled the creation of extremely complex algorithms for encryption, which are almost impossible to decrypt without detailed knowledge of the algorithm or, in some cases, without the actual key used in the encryption.

Cryptography has been used almost since the introduction of the telegraph and is widely used to scramble telephone communications as a protection against wiretapping. Devices now available can be attached between the modem and the compute or terminal. Used in pairs, the sending encryption device translates the text into its encrypted form. The receiving device then translates the encrypted text back into its original form.

A great deal has been written about cryptography as it relates to online communications. However, the majority of a company's data resides on data files stored on tapes and disks resident either in the data centre or at an off-site storage location. There is no reason why sensitive data held on external media should not also be protected by data encryption. Data held on external media are most often held in clear text forms; i.e., assuming that individuals have access to the file, the data are readily accessible and in a readable form. Obviously, not all data maintained would be considered sensitive. It would be the responsibility of individual companies to determine which information, if disclosed, could cause competitive disadvantage, breach of good faith, or other problems.

The organisational structure of the data processing department would have to be expanded to include a data administrator responsible for maintaining an administration data set describing which files within the installation are considered to contain sensitive data. The administration data set would contain each production file deemed to contain sensitive data.

Each entry would contain position and length of the fields to be encrypted/decrypted. Each application would have the facility of specifying a unique key. The job names and passwords which are to be considered as authorised. As each file is opened the administration data set would be accessed using the job name corresponds to an authorised file name as a key. If an entry is found, job name and the correct password is specified; then an indicator within the data control block (DCB) will be set on to indicate that encryption/decryption is required for this file. The remaining pertinent information from the administration data set entry will be stored in core and an address pointer to this information will be stored in the DCB. After each record has been read from the file into core storage, the associated DCB will be interrogated to determine whether any data must be decrypted.

When a record is to be written to an output file, the associated DCB will be interrogated to determine whether any data must be encrypted before being physically written to the output device. The basis of this proposed system lies within the administration data set. Security over the information held within this data set is imperative if the proposed system is to attain the desired level of data security. The data administrator also has a key role in ensuring the completeness, accuracy, and authenticity of the entries within the administration data set. The advantages of this approach to data security are as follows:

i) Actual possession or availability of a production file does not represent an exposure since sensitive information cannot be interpreted.

ii) Sensitive data are made available only in clear text to authorised programmes.

iii) By amending the open, read, and write procedures for all files, the security routines are transparent to individual programmes.

iv) The creation of a data administration function with responsibilities as previously described centralises the responsibility for data privacy and security:

v) The processing overhead will be minimised by determining at open time which files are to be subject to encryption/decryption and by storing all other pertinent information in high-speed core storage.

vi) The data processing department will derive benefit from the standardisation of data protection practices. Test files could-be created directly from production tiles as any sensitive data would be encrypted and therefore not readily available to other than authorised production programmes.

Authentication of online users

An online system must devise alternative methods to identify the person operating the terminal. Once an individual has been accurately identified, it is then possible to restrict that person's access to certain transactions or data files. Identification is usually made by the operator providing some kind of password to the system. The passwords can either be keyed into the system by the operator or can be contained on a badge or card which is inserted into a reader attached to the system.

Access to an online system would consist of two stages. First is the identification stage, where the operator identifies himself to the system. The operator identification can be considered as non-secure information. It may be the surname of the individual, employee account number, or some other type of ID. The second stage concerns the authentication that the operator is who he says he is. This authentication password should be unique to each operator and should be kept confidential.

It is the authentication of identification which has the direct bearing on the security of the system. Some computer packages can generate passwords randomly. User-selected passwords have been found to be the most easily discovered. The following points should be considered when designing controls to protect against unlimited access to an online system.

i) Maintain a password data set identifying authorised personnel who may access the system.
ii) Establish and document the administrative functions responsible for maintenance of this password data set.
iii) Clearly define who has access to this data set and ensure that it is protected from unauthorised disclosure or modification.
iv) Generate passwords randomly by the computer and change as frequently as practicable.
v) Suppress the display or printing of any passwords. In this way it is not possible for anyone to gain knowledge of a password by looking over the shoulder of an operator or by reviewing printed output.
vi) Educate the user to the importance of non-disclosure of passwords and clearly state management policy in the event of unauthorised disclosure.

Various means are being developed for identifying terminal operators by some physical personal characteristic.

It is possible for the owner of a data file to assign a password to the data file at the time of its creation. Access to this file is only available when the password is correctly presented to the system. The advantage of the password system for data file security is that it provides a reasonable level of protection at low cost.

Data files have labels at the beginning and at the end. Part of the information held in the header labels is the date of expiration for the particular file. If an attempt is made to write onto that file prior to the expiration date, a message will appear on the console log. The operator has the option of cancelling the job or of continuing by overriding the date protection.

Where date protection is used as a measure for data security, appropriate administrative controls must be introduced to ensure that only authorised overrides are submitted by the console operator. Reliance on the date protection facility is not a strong control, but it can be strengthened by writing a report to management detailing each system request for date protection override.

Testing

Growing awareness of the need for comprehensive treatment of data security has led to the introduction of several access control software packages designed to protect data from unauthorised disclosure, modification, or destruction, and to permit access to each user on a strict need-to-know basis. Each package has its own features, strengths, and weaknesses.

Before access control software can be introduced, the installation must complete a great deal of pre-planning, including setting up the organisational and administrative function necessary to support the software, classifying users according to what they require access to and classifying data according to its relative need for security. Before new or amended programmes are placed into the production environment, they must be tested using data specially suited to the particular needs of the test.

Testing can be carried out by the programming team responsible for creating or amending the programmes, the user department that will ultimately use the output from the programmes, or the data centre in the form of an acceptance test designed to ensure that the programmes will run successfully in the production environment. The transaction data for the test may be relatively simple to create. In fact, there may not be suitable data on any live transaction files. It may, however, be considered necessary and/or expedient to use a live master file for the test. The increase in the potential for unauthorised modification, disclosure, or destruction of these files is tremendous.

The two well-known testing facilities are regression testing facility and integrated testing facility.

i) *Regression testing facility (RTF)*: A regression testing facility requires setting up a master file and transaction file containing all known conditions. Each record is documented, stating the content of the record and its purpose during the running of a test. The documentation for the transaction file should also contain a section on the expected results after application of the transaction. Tests of the system are run using these files. Whenever the system is changed, the tests can be rerun and the two sets of output compared. Output results can be compared either visually, which can be a long, tedious, error-prone task, or by the use of an automated file-compare facility. The regression testing facility requires a high degree of documentation and a commitment to keep both the documentation and the files in line with the current production environment.

ii) *Integrated test facility (ITF)*: An integrated test facility entails the incorporation of certain records into the live master file for use as a testing vehicle. Tests are conducted using these, records, and they can be created and amended according to the needs of the test. The main advantages of an integrated test facility are in problem determination, auditability, and training.

a) Where an error condition is suspected, the condition can be recreated in a live situation without affecting the authentic records oil the file.

b) The auditors have the opportunity of submitting transactions for processing by the production system in its production environment without disrupting the run.

c) Employees training on the system can use these dummy records until the have sufficient knowledge to work on the authentic records.

An ITF combined with a regression testing facility can provide a powerful tool in ensuring that systems are properly tested prior to their introduction into the production environment.

Employee Education

The ultimate aim of any security education programme is to familiarise personnel with existing security safeguards, including why safeguards are employed, what safeguards are designed to protect against, how these safeguards work, and what is the result of utilising each safeguard. Further, this education programme should bring about a general attitude of security awareness on the part of all personnel:

i) Awareness of what security problems exist and what opportunities for improvement are available.

ii) Awareness of the employee's own security responsibilities as well as those of his co-workers.

iii) Awareness of what to do when security violations are detected.

The security requirements of the company should be clearly stated in writing and readily available to all employees. New employees should be made aware of the company requirements and requested to read the appropriate documentation. Existing employees should be given refresher courses and also kept up-to-date with any enhancements or changes in the security programme. A possible method of ensuring that employees are periodically reminded of the security requirements is to ask them to complete a staff declaration to the effect that they are aware of the security requirements and have no knowledge of any breach in them.

COMPUTER CRIME INVESTIGATION

Information may be stored on computer media such as tapes or discs, or in solid state circuitry devices. When an investigation begins, the investigator should become familiar with the suspect document or source programmes. The chain of evidence in computer crime cases is as critical as in any crime case, and because of the necessary evidence safeguards that must be provided, such as special temperatures for the storing of discs or tapes, it is important to document each move and the individual handling of evidence. Computer crimes are difficult cases to develop and solve and may require many more resources than most organisations have at the disposal. It is important to develop a good investigatic methodology so that case work will follow smoothly.

The perpetrator of a computer fraud has a need to fulfil or a problem to solve. He discovers assets associated with a computer system to satisfy the need or to solve the problem, generates an idea for action, and rationalises the justification for it. The first decision of the perpetrator is whether or not an accomplice will be needed to carry out the plan. If needed, they will have to be brought into the plans. When these people have been identified, the perpetrators must acquire the necessary skills, knowledge and access to the computer system that is to be attacked. Plans must be drawn up and tested. If the plans are inadequate, additional accomplices may have to be brought in. Once the plans are complete, the fraud is executed. There is always the possibility that the act is observed by witnesses. This heightens the prospect of detection. If the act is not detected, there is no further action and the perpetrator has accomplished the fraud. If it is detected but the perpetrator is not exposed, the fraud has still been accomplished.

The investigator should:

a) interview all possible sources of information such as data processing personnel, security staff, building maintenance personnel and all individuals with access to the scene of the crime. If the computer system is a network or a distributed system each phase of the investigation must be repeated at each site.

b) establish an estimate, or an exact amount, of loss to determine whether or not the case should be handled by the corporate policy.

c) determine the organisation's policy towards prosecuting an employee for internal theft.

d) determine if civil law suits exist, are pending, or are being contemplated by the organisation, in the case about to be investigated.

e) determine whether the organisation has begun an internal investigation.

f) contact expert witnesses you may need for the investigation, such as programmers, systems analysts, auditors, etc. The flow of information and data always follows the same basic path: manual, input, processing, and output. Determine by investigation at which point the crime occurred and track both ways to set up an audit trail.

g) secure the documentation for prosecution and, if necessary, lock up tapes, discs, printouts, etc. Be aware of special storage requirements for individual items, that is, temperature, humidity, dust, etc.

h) formulate your case theory; identify possible suspects and facts as they emerge for case analysis and preparation. Be flexible in your case theory, be prepared to alter it as new information is uncovered.

i) compile all evidence, testimony, documents, sketches, photographs, etc., related to the case.

A good risk management system requires a high level of personal involvement and participation from senior management, who have to play a major role in deciding on the levels of risks which are acceptable to the organisation. This could be achieved by carrying out a corporate security review and a corporate loss assessment on the company's computer services to users. The corporate security review examines computer-processed information as a corporate asset to identify the risks of unavailability, errors and omissions, abuse, unauthorised disclosure, and to determine their potential implications.

Each risk should be assessed in terms of the likely probability of occurrence and severity of loss or damage incurred. The corporate loss assessment examines key individual business systems to identify and, where appropriate, quantify losses to the company arising from both short-term and long-term disruption of computer facilities. Often the extent of business interruption losses arising from malicious damage or arson attacks would far outweigh losses from equipment damage.

Clerical recovery in business areas could also take much longer than the recovery of computer service in the company. Business interruption losses could accrue from any of the following eventualities:

a) Cash-flow delays through late invoicing.
b) Production delays from shortage of raw materials through inability to pay suppliers for previous deliveries.
c) Stock shortage or overstocking of raw materials and finished goods through poor stock control.
d) Bad business decisions through lack of planning tools, or erroneous information produced by computer systems.
e) Late delivery through missing shipping schedules and operational inefficiency.
f) Missing peak-sale periods for seasonal goods where the loss of business may be irretrievable.

g) Loss of new business and investments through late entry of new products on the market arising from delays in research and development programmes.

h) Loss of new and existing customers through erosion of market leadership, competitiveness in pricing and product availability.

i) Loss of profits through having to sell indirectly via wholesalers, instead of direct deliveries to retailers, and/or inability to exploit marginal trading opportunities.

j) Loss of goodwill to customers, staff and third parties.

k) Loss of public confidence leading to permanent damage to business or technical defaults.

l) Payments of fines through failure to comply with trade regulations and government legislation.

m) Payment of damages to customers and third parties, through delays in completion of work and failure to meet specifications or quality control standards.

The cost of implementing various direct countermeasures has to be balanced against the various levels of probable direct and consequential losses. Nevertheless, risk reduction measures may be examined in detail to reduce the frequency of occurrence, as well as the severity of loss. Probable risks with high loss or catastrophic business impact must be avoided, otherwise the business would not remain viable. Several options are open for positive action: reduction or prevention; detection; response; and recovery. These are implemented through installation of protection equipment and software, appointment of control and security personnel, setting up control and reporting procedures, or providing security training to improve general awareness of risks, and taking effective action to minimise losses.

Risk prevention measures are applied to reduce the likelihood of occurrence of risks, or to reduce the extent of loss or damage sustained by the company. Taking the example of physical damage by fire, arson or explosion, the installation of access-control systems to safeguard premises and computer installations would reduce the likelihood of terrorists or undesirable parties entering the premises to start a fire or plant a bomb. The installation of automatic halon or carbon dioxide fire protection systems would reduce fire damage by fast response and effective control. Partitioning off areas containing high value equipment, using fire resistant material, will reduce fire spread and localise fire damage. Early detection followed by effective action would help to contain losses in a local area.

Computer rooms are mostly fitted with smoke detection equipment in the room, floor void and ceiling void to allow early detection of fire hasards. The sophisticated computer auditor could design fraud-detection computer models to facilitate policing of the company's business transactions by spotting abnormal activities quickly and taking action to curtail further damage to the company. Regular review of job reruns and system access violation would help to pinpoint the various causes of errors and omissions or potential abuse, and would help determine appropriate corrective action to enhance operation performance and data integrity. Proper procedures in response to deliberate or accidental physical damage and cautious handling of fraud or theft cases could both act as an effective deterrent against similar future offences, and may reduce losses by proper salvage actions or recovery of lost monies or property from guilty parties. Adequate preplanning of recovery from major disasters would help to speed up the resumption of normal working through systematic and coordinated action, resulting in reduction of business interruption losses.

For the last 10 years, large companies have become increasingly aware of their heavy dependence on computing in business functions. As a result, more and more data processing installations are now equipped with backup and stand-by provisions, together with a set of contingency action plans to deal with various forms of computer disasters. The frauds were successful because the victim companies failed to appreciate the need for proper segregation of duties in key functions. Some small companies or installations could ill afford the luxury of separate manning for input, data control, system design, programming and computer operation. As more small business computers come into use in individual business departments and inadequate attention is given to the control and auditability of business applications, more organisations fall prey to clandestine activities by rogue staff who hold key positions in data processing in what used to be traditional user departments.

Computer security programmes are necessary to increase the security awareness of staff. Some proprietary packaged systems offer little or no safeguards against unauthorised access to business data and software. An unattended office computer can be easily powered up, the database compromised, and the system powered down, all within a matter of minutes, and no one may ever find out that damage was done. The role of internal auditors in combating computer fraud becomes more urgent as the number of potential perpetrators with the necessary computing skills grows with the proliferation of personal computers.

Sharing of computer skills among more business users would facilitate the introduction of proper job rotation for sensitive duties and dual control of sensitive tasks. Financial institutions are increasingly aware of the potential for frauds in electronic funds transfer systems. This is evidenced by increasing demands for BIS computer fraud surveys from insurance underwriters who wish to provide banks with cover against high value frauds. Several pilot schemes are also underway among clearing banks wishing to gain first-hand experience with encryption devices, with the view to adopting these in electronic funds transfer (EFT) systems to provide better protection for financial transactions transmitted across national boundaries.

The countermeasures for effective control against computer fraud can be broadly categorised into the following strategy: prevention or reduction; detection; and response.

The strategy of employing counter-measures is to prevent a fraud occurring. Should this become highly counter-productive or too expensive to implement, the alternative strategy would be to adopt measures to make it difficult to carry out the abuse, in order to either reduce the frequency of occurrence or minimise the takings. By far the most effective control is to reduce the ability of one individual to exercise control in more than one functional area. For example, the function of placing orders for goods or service from outside the company should be different from that of checking for goods received, as well as authorising for payment. Independent checking by different individuals in different areas would render the concealment of a fraud and the realisation of gains impossible without collusion. The more widespread collusion is needed to make a scheme work, the less likely it is that a fraud will succeed, and the easier it is to detect the abuse.

Computer frauds involve exploiting loopholes in input and output controls. Try to make it difficult for an unauthorised person to intercept or tamper with submission of input and collection of output. The data control function should be separate from data preparation. Proper access control should be enforced on remote terminals to prevent culprits from abusing unattended terminals used for data or input modification. Attention should be given to the administration and control of the use of passwords. Terminal users should be made aware of the importance of the safe custody of their passwords or identity codes. The use of data encryption for data transmission on public networks would gain increasing popularity as an effective deterrent against wiretappers.

Proper authorisation procedures should and programmers make changes to live systems and data. Where possible there should be independent checking of the amendments to make sure no illegal codes or unauthorised amendments have been included in the process. The amended programme should be tested before the live version is replaced. A structured walk-through in system design enables the details of a computer system to be known to more than one individual. Auditors should be involved in system design and acceptance testing to plug possible loopholes in control procedures and identify target areas in the system where abuse could be perpetrated.

The system and programme documentation should be of a high standard to make it possible for an independent person to maintain the system. If the system designer is the only person who understands the system and therefore the only person who can maintain it, the company would be relying heavily on that person's integrity or loyalty. There should be proper rotation of duties in the organisation to ensure a person does not remain entrenched in a particular function or position. Boredom and frustration could cause an individual to test the system's weakness, as a technical challenge, and then to exploit this knowledge for private gains. When a sensitive task is carried out, make sure that the joint effort of at least two persons is required to fulfil that task. For example, a cheque would only be valid if it was endorsed by two different signatures. Abuse would be difficult unless both parties are in collusion. The use of digital electronic signatures, making use of private and public keys for data encryption and decryption respectively, should be considered in EFT applications over an international network.

It is difficult to differentiate between a deliberate abuse and a genuine error. If the perpetrator was challenged, he would excuse himself for having made a mistake. Where possible, an organisation should issue clear instructions to staff that certain practices are forbidden, e.g., a document marked secret must not be removed from the premises or programmers not allowed to enter the computer room, and management will regard any rule breaking as extremely serious.

Bona fide references should always be followed up with new recruits, especially temporary or contract staff. Employees should be regularly appraised to monitor staff morale or to resolve grievances. Proper job motivation and career development should be provided in addition to adequate remuneration and proper merit awards to encourage productivity and staff contribution. Termination procedures should be strict but fair. Employees dismissed for gross misconduct or incompetence should be escorted out of the premises when notice is given and denied access to computer facilities or remote terminals.

If management are worried about possible losses from abuse despite having provided reasonable safeguards, then insurance cover should be provided on fidelity guarantee for both accounting and computer staff to ameliorate any future loss through fraud or embezzlement. Computer crime insurance cover is also available from major insurers against high value frauds running into millions of pounds.

Detection of potential abuse would serve to reduce corporate losses arising from such abuse. Effective monitoring would also deter potential perpetrators from attempting to experiment with illegal schemes, if the risk of detection was high. Illegal attempts to gain access into sensitive areas, i.e., trespassing, or guessing at passwords in order to sign on or access files from remote terminals, should be logged and reviewed regularly. One effective detection of hacking activities is to display the last log-on time and date on the screen after the user has successfully logged on to the system. Statistics of access violation should be collected with regard to details of the particular terminals being abused and the files being accessed. The results should be reviewed by someone with security responsibility.

Any unusual spending habits of staff, especially if extravagant lifestyles or expensive hobbies suggest that individuals may be living beyond their means, pay attention to staff who may be financially embarrassed or running into serious domestic problems. Beware of unsupervised work, especially if the person regularly volunteered for overtime working and was allowed to stay on the premises unsupervised. Several frauds came to light when the perpetrators failed to cover their trail whilst away on holiday leave. Adequate audit trails should be provided for computer systems to highlight and locate areas of errors and abuse. Exception reports should be regularly monitored and reviewed.

Computer auditors in several breweries and oil companies have successfully developed computer audit programmes to detect fraud. The objective of computer modelling is to bring to light significant variations in business patterns from the normal population monitored in the industry. For example, say the model highlighted that the relative sales figures of various grades of petrol or various forms of beer over a period from an outlet differed significantly from other outlets. The business activities of that outlet would be investigated to look for possible abuse by the proprietor.

In some cases the culprit was being allowed to perpetrate the same abuse on change of employment because the former employer failed to alert the new employer of his misdeeds. The culprit was simply dismissed or allowed to resign and then the whole affair hushed up. When there is adequate evidence collected for conviction, the perpetrator should always be prosecuted. This would act as a serious warning to others contemplating making similar attempts and can be extremely effective as a deterrent.

LIBRARY MANAGEMENT SYSTEM (LMS)

Today, the security of the programmes developed to process these data will be considered. It is essential that the application programmes executed in the production environment be authorised, meet the criteria for which they were designed, and not perform any additional unauthorised functions. An effective Library Management System (LMS), therefore, consists of the administrative and logical controls to ensure that new or amended library members to be migrated into the production environment are authorised, properly documented signed-off by the appropriate parties, and, once in the production environment, are protected from unauthorised activity. There should be a distinction between the environment in which this programme is created and the environment in which the programme will be used to process live data.

Where control over production data files limits access to production programmes, the LMS need only secure the contents of the production programme libraries. Before any programme can be migrated into the production environment, it must be thoroughly tested to ensure that it does what it was designed to do and nothing more. After a programme has been migrated into the production environment, the LMS must protect this member against unauthorised changes. That it is the source statement library and the executable library members which are migrated into the production environment after they have been adequately tested. In some installations there may be an intermediate set of libraries from which the user testing and data centre acceptance testing would be executed.

To ensure the integrity of the programmes being tested, the programmers would not have access to these intermediate libraries. The following is a list of considerations to be made in the development of an effective library management system:

i) Determine what libraries require protection. If production data cannot be accessed from test libraries, the level of protection afforded to these libraries may be minimal.

ii) Back-up and recovery procedures should be designed to counter a partial or total loss of the libraries.

iii) Changes to protected libraries should be authorised by the user department serviced by the programmes. This aspect provides for segregation of duties and prevents any programmer from submitting an unauthorised change through established channels.

iv) An audit trail should be made of changes to source statements in order that such changes can easily be verified to the change that was authorised.

v) There should be a way of ascertaining that the most recent version of the executable programme corresponds to the most recent version of the related source statements.

vi) After the programmer has finished testing a programme in the testing environment, there should be a method of freezing the source and executable code while user and data centre testing is carried out.

vii) Actual changes to the production libraries should be effected by data centre personnel, thereby providing an additional level of security through enhanced segregation of duties.

viii) The documentation supporting any activity to these production libraries should be complete and contain provision for the appropriate sign-offs indicating that the programmes may form an authorised part of the production environment. The archival system supported by the LMS should provide for adequate recovery facilities should a new version of a programme fail to work in production.

ix) Management should receive reports from the LMS indicating activity against the protected libraries and also noting any unauthorised accesses, whether they resulted in a change being made or not.

x) Management should have a clearly defined policy in the event of any unauthorised activity regarding these libraries.

xi) Provision should be made for controlling the implementation of emergency changes. Emergency changes are usually made because of the discovery of an error in a programme running in production. Time constraints usually do not allow emergency changes to go through the normal channels of authorisation, testing, and sign-off. For these reasons, emergency changes must have special provisions for follow-up after the change has been implemented. On no account should emergency changes be accepted as a normal part of the operational environment.

It is the duty of the auditor to assess the adequacy, effectiveness, and efficiency of the system of internal control within an organisation. Until the introduction of computer systems on a large scale, the auditor's role in an organisation was fairly well defined. In recent years however, an increasing reliance upon computer systems has forced the auditor to adjust to a new environment. To adequately fulfil his primary function, the auditor must have access to a great deal of information not normally available to one individual. This information will include details of all the data security measures in force within an installation.

An organisation must, therefore, have a degree of protection against any unauthorised activities by its auditors, and the auditors, while still maintaining their independence, must be protected from unwarranted suspicion should an exposure occur. The auditor's role in a computer environment has been the topic of a great deal of discussion and controversy. The main issue is the question of involvement and the maintenance of the auditor's independence.

On the one hand is the argument that if the auditor is actively involved in the design stages of a system, he will not be able to present an unbiased assessment of the controls within the system and may be at a disadvantage if a weakness is subsequently highlighted. The other side of the argument is that computer systems are substantially different in their approach to security and require the auditor to grow with the system if he is to attest to the adequacy of the controls built into the system.

6
Preservation

Preservation of a library's collection is as important as the acquisition of the collection. Morrow defined preservation as "The action taken to prevent, stop or retard deterioration: 'conservation' means maintaining in usable condition, each item in the collection; and 'restoration' implies returning the deteriorated item to its original or near-original condition. 'Information preservation' as opposed to preservation of the physical object, consists of reformatting materials in order to preserve their intellectual content." Morrow provides an excellent outline of what might be included in a policy statement and also guidelines for organising a preservation department.

A formal, well-prepared policy statement will, therefore, provide the guidelines necessary for the implementation and carrying out of a preservation programme. Like book selection policy statements, the preservation statement should be broadly based and developed with the input of the entire library staff. Preservation policy will affect every library department and future service to library patrons.

The scope, goals, financial resources of the library's programme are major determining factors in establishing a preservation department. Each library should have a preservation officer, full-or part-time as dictated by the size and scope of the library's collections. In research libraries the staff might include a head of preservation and subunits, each with necessary staff. Staffing a preservation department requires careful recruiting. It may be necessary to assign present, interested staff and provide in-house and workshop or intern training at another institution to initially establish a preservation department or programme.

A fully organised preservation department will need an administrator with experience or training in preservation practices. Other staff will need appropriate education and training in relevant conservation or microfilming laboratories, binderies, etc., to fulfil their job responsibilities. Preservation policy makes sense only if it is technically and economically realistic, so that until a library or archive knows the extent of its own preservation needs it cannot usefully determine what its policy shall be.

The preservation problem arises from two fundamental physical causes: first, there are the inherent properties and weaknesses of the materials used as information media; and secondly, we must consider the interaction between the materials and the environment in which they are stored and used.

ENVIRONMENTAL ENEMIES

The environmental enemies of books are conventionally classified under five broad headings:

i) temperature.
ii) humidity.
iii) light.
iv) biological infestation.
v) pollution.

Temperature

The tolerance of human beings for temperature variations is fairly limited. The full range of temperatures known to scientists is from absolute zero to the alleged temperature at the centre of the sun. In practice people can survive only in a minute part of this range, from about –10°C to about 50°C. Human tolerance is slightly increased by the use of special clothing and equipment, but, in effect, beyond these limits a person can survive only by carrying a micro-environment in the form of a completely enclosed suit of some kind and adequate supplies of air.

Modern technology has given us far greater control over the internal environment of buildings. We can regulate the air temperature to within one or two degrees, and it can be monitored so that it remains roughly constant even if extreme changes take place outside the building. This capacity is a fairly new phenomenon. If central heating has increased the temperature in buildings in temperate countries, air-conditioning has had the opposite effect in hot climates. Of course, hundreds of millions of people lived in the very hot parts of the globe long before any artificial cooling systems were available, and indeed they still do so where such systems are not in use.

Modern library buildings have central heating systems or air-conditioning systems incorporated in the design, and many older buildings have had such systems installed. The results are generally very pleasant for staff and users. For the books they have been catastrophic. The basic scientific reason for this catastrophe can be stated very simply. The speed of chemical reactions increases with rises in temperature. First, the acid in the paper reacts with such catalysts as atmospheric pollutants or the water content in the air; this breaks down the cellulose which bonds together the fibres in the paper. Secondly, a process of oxidation can take place in certain circumstances, especially with prolonged exposure to light, in which residual metals in the paper will degrade both the lignin and the cellulose, and hence weaken the chemical structure of the paper. Such processes of degradation can be inhibited or delayed by controlling other environmental conditions, but high temperatures will always exacerbate the effects of all the inherent chemical problems of paper, even in high-quality 'acid-free' or chemically inert paper.

There is no 'ideal' temperature for paper, and for the cheap acidic paper which was used for so many nineteenth- and early twentieth-century books and documents no regulation of temperature can prevent inevitable eventual destruction. However, it is possible to delay the inevitable by careful temperature controls, and to do so within limits which are broadly acceptable to both staff and users. One crucial point is that changes in temperature are, if anything, more damaging than a consistently high temperature. Thus to move a book from a coolish air-conditioned store to a heated reading room can do more damage than to have the storage area slightly overheated.

In broad terms, paper will tolerate a temperature of about 20-22°C, provided that the air is fairly dry. This is acceptable to people, and attainable in most buildings in which the ambient temperature can be regulated. The relevant British Standard suggests that the temperature for the storage of paper and parchment in archives should be in the three-range 13-18°C. In practice, this can be attained only for rarely-used materials in storage areas in which there is only an occasional human presence, since such a temperature would now be regarded as being too 'cold' for a working environment.

In practice, paper is quite tolerant within these broad limits. For non-paper media, storage temperatures are far more critical. For example, modern PVC gramophone records can, in theory, tolerate up to about 50°C, but in practice begin to warp at a considerably lower temperature if they are consistently stored in such heat. In practice, about 20°C, with as little variation as possible, is recommended.

Electronic and magnetic media are even more sensitive. The magnetic media, both audio tape and the magnetic discs and tapes used for the storage of digitised data outside a computer, also need to be kept at constant and controlled temperatures. Humidity control is probably even more important than simple temperature control in these cases. Indeed, problems of long-term preservation of these media are still unsolved, and at present they can really be regarded only as temporary storage systems.

Data which exist only on magnetic media need to be regularly copied in order to ensure their long-term survival without degradation. Optical discs, and the technologically similar compact audio discs, seem to have greater potential as long-term preservation media, being more tolerant of their ambient environment, although the testing procedures which have been used to establish their lifetimes seem to be open to some question.

Photographic film is the most sensitive medium of all. The maximum temperature at which celluloid film can be stored for archival purposes is 21°C, and it has very little tolerance of temperature change. More than ±4°C will cause near-fatal problems, so that a constant temperature is more than merely an ideal if the objective is long-term preservation.

Humidity

Humidity can be defined as the percentage of the quantity of water in a particular volume of air in relation to the maximum quantity which it can hold at its present temperature. The natural range of relative humidity (RH) in buildings in temperate countries is probably between about 30 per cent and 60 per cent. However, the RH can be modified by mechanical devices.

Dehumidifiers remove excess moisture from the air, and can be used on a very small scale, or on a large scale throughout a building as part of an air-conditioning system. To solve the opposite problem, humidifiers can increase the moisture levels in very dry air. Air-conditioning systems normally incorporate humidity controls, so that in practice humidity and temperature are regulated together. To human beings, the perceptions of humidity and temperature are closely associated; there is indeed a scientific link between them. High temperatures and high levels of RH are perhaps the least comfortable circumstances in which we normally find ourselves. We also find combinations of high RH and low temperatures; this is the condition loosely called 'damp' by most people. More rarely, we encounter the high temperatures and low RH associated with the Middle East or the American south-west.

In order to create a fully controlled environment, an air-conditioning system has to be able to regulate both temperature and humidity to pre-determined levels. The 'wrong' RH can lead to serious and irreversible damage to paper and other information storage materials. Briefly, if conditions are too dry, paper will become embrittled, while if they are too damp, fungal moulds will develop.

The opposite extreme of very dry conditions generally exists only in hot desert areas. Libraries have been established in such regions only recently, and, like other buildings, are typically equipped with excellent air-conditioning systems. Provided the system is functioning properly, there is no serious problem of dryness inside the building.

It is the excessively damp conditions which are both more common and more problematical. The basic physical facts can be stated simply. The moisture in the air will be partially transferred to all absorbent substances with which it is in contact. It is a particular problem of handmade paper, in whose manufacture the drying process was generally less effective than the artificial heat used in Fourdrinier machines.

Dampness is a major problem for libraries and archives in many parts of the world, and especially for the great historic research libraries and archival repositories of Europe. Their massive collections on handmade paper are in serious danger from mould damage if climatic conditions are not properly controlled. In temperate climates, and especially in north-west Europe, dampness is often found in the older buildings in which many major libraries and repositories are still housed.

Buildings are inevitably subject to dampness after centuries of existence and because some of them are, quite rightly, historic monuments as well as working libraries there may even be legal limits within which any structural alterations or visible modifications have to take place. Many smaller collections, such as those of cathedrals or country houses, are housed in similar buildings, with the added complication that in some cases their owners are unable to bear the considerable costs of whatever environmental improvements might be achieved.

Mould can and does develop in cold and damp conditions, and dehumidification is essential if serious trouble is to be avoided. Once microbiological damage takes place it can rarely be reversed. The humidity problem in tropical and subtropical regions is even more dramatic, if only because it is universal. Heat and humidity promote the development of moulds at an uncontrollable rate, and libraries and archives in such places face a major difficulty. This is exacerbated when, as is the case in many developing countries, funds cannot be made available from limited national resources for the installation and very heavy running costs of elaborate air-conditioning systems.

In any case, many collections have spent decades or even centuries in unsuitable conditions before they ever reach the comparative safety of a public repository. Control can only be achieved by eliminating the worst affected materials, which may at least prevent the further spread of mould, and then by creating a micro-climate in which materials of exceptional importance can be housed. Mould growth takes place at any temperature in a range from 15 to 35°C, although it seems to be at its worst at about 30°C.

There is a similarly wide range of RH levels at which mould growth will occur in higher temperatures, from about 45 per cent to about 60 per cent, although laboratory experiments suggest that, fortunately, development is at its worst only when an exceptionally high 75 per cent of RH is reached. There is a direct and significant relationship between temperature change and the moisture levels in hygroscopic materials. As warm air is cooled, it deposits some of its moisture content, which is absorbed by any hygroscopic materials with which it comes into contact. Thus, cooling the air by 4°C can raise the RH by as much as 10 per cent. In other words, if the temperature is to be controlled by reducing it to acceptable levels for books and users alike, the RH must also be controlled to ensure that the books do not absorb the surplus moisture which the air extrudes as the temperature falls. This is a particular problem in tropical countries, where RH is naturally about 60 per cent for much of the time, and the temperature an uncomfortable 30°C or more.

It is even more difficult to define an 'ideal' RH than it is to define an 'ideal' temperature. Indeed the two cannot in practice be wholly disentangled. Where a full environmental control system is available, the recommended level of RH for a library is between 55 per cent and 65 per cent, provided that the temperature is held between 13 and 18°C. It is doubtful whether this counsel of perfection can be attained in most libraries, but ensuring a constant RH, at a reasonable level, is probably more important than absolute precision in attaining an ideal percentage.

Maintaining an acceptable level of RH is important for paper and parchment, but, as with temperature levels, for photographic materials it is critical. Moulds can develop on photographic film, while the paper on which prints are made is, of course, subject to the same problems as other paper. For film, however, a much more important problem is that a constantly high level of RH will break down the gelatin size which is used as a divider between the layers of chemical of which film consists. An RH of 60 per cent is the absolute maximum permissible for film storage and use, even if only short-term preservation is envisaged.

For long-term preservation of archival master negatives of research materials, it is almost impossible for the RH to be too low. In practice, a range of 15 per cent to 40 per cent is acceptable for monochrome microfilm, and up to 50 per cent for other monochrome films. For colour films and diazo films, however, the upper limit is substantially lower, being no more than 30 per cent. In fact, for long-term security, storage at near-zero temperature and RH is probably the best method, the ideal combination being perhaps 2°C and two per cent RH.

Light

The damage inflicted on paper by excessive light is chemical. Ultraviolet radiation, found both in sunlight and in artificial fluorescent light, contributes to the breakdown of the cellulose structures in the paper. It is also the direct cause of the fading of pigments of inks and of dyes in colour film and photographic prints. Direct sunlight raises the air temperature, especially if it passes through glass, and all conventional artificial lighting systems generate some heat which radiates from the light source.

The ideal level of lighting for the storage of library materials of all kinds is total darkness, but it is only in closed stack areas this can be attained. It is a sensible economy measure, quite apart from being desirable, to ensure that closed-access stacks are lit only when they are in use by book fetchers, except for the any legally required minimum level of emergency or security lighting. Stack lighting, consisting of fluorescent tubes fitted with ultraviolet filters and diffusers, presents no real preservation problems if it is sensibly and economically used. Reading areas are more difficult. Readers need appropriate levels of light for working. For areas in which old or fragile materials are used, fluorescent lighting, with ultraviolet filters, is probably the most suitable system, and is certainly the cheapest to operate. If there are windows in reading areas or stacks, it is essential that they too have ultraviolet filters in or on the glass. As in so many other aspects of preservation, we have to be realistic and sensible about this.

Libraries cannot expect users or staff to work in Stygian gloom. The ultimate objective of preservation is to facilitate, not to inhibit, the use of materials, but to do so in circumstances which are consistent with the continued existence of the materials themselves. Moderate but acceptable levels of filtered light will achieve precisely this. Monochrome film which has been processed to archival standards suffers little from light. Colour film, transparencies and prints, however, are very sensitive. Theoretically, this could be a serious obstacle to preservation, and certainly should be considered in, for example, planning to use first-generation colour photographs in a long-term exhibition.

Biological Infestation

Paper is subject to biological infestation by mould spores and by insects which are attracted to the its chemical constituents as a medium for growth or as food. Mould has already been mentioned in considering the problems arising from excessive humidity.

Insect infestation needs to be considered separately. While this is a problem which is at its worst in libraries and archives in tropical countries, it is certainly not unique to them. Indeed, various silverfish, cockroaches and so-called 'bookworms' are comparatively common, especially in older buildings in temperate countries. The various species of insects have slightly different tastes; some prefer paper, while some choose to dine off binding adhesives or even sewing threads. Some particularly fastidious gourmets select a particular kind of paper, such as 'art' paper with a high china clay content in its glazed surface.

The elimination of insect infestation is an expensive undertaking for which outside specialists would normally have to be employed. As always in library preservation, prevention is better than having to find—and to fund—a cure. A number of comparatively simple measures can dramatically reduce the likelihood of insect problems. The elimination of vegetable matter from the library and its outer walls is one factor. Planters and flower displays inside, and creepers growing on the outside walls, may be aesthetically pleasing, but they encourage insects.

The proper care of all the wooden parts of the library, whether structural or in the form of furniture or shelving, is also critical, since termites breed in wood. It is particularly important in tropical countries to ensure that, as far as possible, the library building is inaccessible not only to termites, but also to cockroaches and to the rodents which inevitably abound in such climates. The well-sealed buildings with which we are familiar in temperate regions are neither normal nor indeed climatically necessary in hotter countries, especially where air-conditioning is not an economic possibility. The only option open to the librarian or archivist in such circumstances is to ensure that the books and documents are regularly monitored.

i) *Insects*: There are more than 70 varieties of insects that can be destructive to library materials. The most common are cockroaches, silverfish, termites, book lice, bookworms, mud wasps, and moths. The problem of insects is less of a problem in the continental United States, particularly in the northern states, than in many other parts of the world. Problems with insects are particularly acute in tropical and subtropical climates. Poor housekeeping, excessive moisture, darkness, etc., may all contribute to insect problems.

   Insects should generally not be a problem in newer libraries, with modern buildings equipped with air-conditioning or ventilation systems, temperature control, and proper lighting. There are hundreds of species of cockroaches, but only a few pose a problem for libraries. They are most commonly found in tropical and subtropical climates and attack paste and glue in book covers. They excrete a dark liquid that discolours pages or other objects over which they crawl.

Silverfish, like cockroaches, are attracted to glue and paste and will eat through covers to get at adhesives. They thrive in cool, damp areas and are generally not a problem in dry, well-ventilated places or among books in frequent use. Termites are more common in tropical and subtropical climates but also appear even in far northern climates. They eat cellulose and will attack all papers. Termites can be difficult to detect because they eat into the interior of objects, leaving only an outer shell. Book lice, also called psocids, occur frequently in old, damp, musty volumes. They thrive best in warm, damp rooms that are not often disturbed. 'Bookworm' is a generic term for hundreds of beetles found throughout the world. They lay their eggs on the outer edges of books; after hatching, the larvae eat (tunnel) into the pages and covers.

Cleanliness, awareness, and periodic inspections easily control insects and that they can be eradicated by fumigation or the application of insecticides. Good housekeeping practices are most important, including the removal of food residues that attract insects.

ii) *Rodents*: Rodents can potentially be a problem in libraries. Rats and mice can do tremendous damage to stored papers and books. Proper housekeeping practices and eradication programmes should eliminate this potential problem altogether.

iii) *Fungi*: Fungi are a major problem in tropical and subtropical climates with high temperature, and high humidity. The problem will not occur in well-ventilated or air-conditioned libraries. Damage can be extensive, but the spores an be killed through proper conservation treatment.

Pollution

The pollution of the environment has, of course, become a major political issue in many countries during the last decade, and some small steps are being taken to alleviate it. Nevertheless, it is, and will continue to be, a serious danger to both life and property, especially in heavily populated urban areas. Atmospheric pollution has been a consequence of industri-alisation ever since man first made fire and filled his cave with smoke. It is unavoidable in the modern world, and all we can do is try to contain it at acceptable levels and deal with the consequences of what remains.

The major pollutant in industrialised countries was in the form of the sulphur products of coal burning. For more than a century, coal was the principal fuel for transport, machinery, heating and the generation of other forms of power such as gas and electricity. The effects of various pollutants on library and archival materials can be very severe indeed. At the simplest level, dirt is not only unsightly but damaging. Particles of dust can cause physical damage to paper. If the RH is high, the dust may become even more hygroscopic than the paper and consequently accelerate the degradation of the cellulose structure.

The dust and dirt particles are themselves chemicals which may, for example, contain fragments of lead from combusted petrol or alkaline dust from cement on a building site. Each particular kind of 'dust' sets up its own chemical reactions, although the general effects are the same, and they are all almost equally deleterious. Oxidation by sulphur dioxide or carbon monoxide can break down cellulose and hence exacerbate the deterioration of paper and parchment. Not all such chemical pollutants are external to the materials themselves. Some synthetic polymers, used in films, magnetic tape and indeed in paper, may contain minute quantities of chemical impurities which can lead to internal breakdown of the molecular structure. This is fortunately avoidable and rare, for the use of high-quality film and tape effectively eliminates this particular hazard.

The control of the air quality in a library building is important for people as well as materials. A fully functional air-conditioning system is the ideal solution, since it will filter and purify the air as well as control the temperature and humidity. Where this is not practicable for the whole building, it may be possible to create smaller controlled environments, such as a room or even a cupboard, for materials of exceptional importance or great vulnerability. Security copies of computer tapes, for example, are normally stored in a completely controlled environment.

A library may well feel that the master copy of its catalogue deserves this treatment in view of the cost of replacement in case of loss or damage. More traditionally, a book or manuscript of exceptional value might be exhibited to the public only in an environmentally controlled display case. Control of the external environment is ultimately beyond the power of the librarian or archivist, but it is necessary to be aware of it, especially if there are any hazards and sudden changes such as construction work. Those ideal conditions can conflict both with what is attainable and indeed with what is acceptable to those people who use and work with the collections.

Cultural heritage objects, or historical research materials of great importance, whose physical preservation is deemed to be essential, will have to be protected more stringently. Indeed, they may be made available to users only in surrogate form or under very carefully controlled conditions. In some cases, the information medium itself may dictate the conditions in which it is kept. Colour film and magnetic tape, for example, both require special conditions if their useful life is to be maximised, and the tolerances for these media are far more critical the those for paper or parchment. However, the basic principles of physical conservation are clear enough. A building which is clean, dry and no overheated will not destroy its contents. The design, use and maintenance of the building is an integral part of a preservation programme, for those factors effectively define the immediate environment in which the materials are stored and, in the case of non-circulating collections, used.

In the inevitably rare circumstance of a new building being planned, the librarian or archivist will wish to ensure that the basic design is conceived with the preservation of materials in mind. Where funding is available, full environmental controls throughout the building are the ideal, although it has to be remembered that the functioning of the building, the maintenance of its contents and the comfort of its staff and users then become wholly dependent upon the efficient operation of that system. A poor installation, or one which frequently breaks down, is worse than none at all.

In countries with unreliable power supplies, for example, or where spare parts or skilled labour for repair work may be in short supply, adaptations of traditional local building designs can sometimes be far better than a Western-style building. High ceilings, with or without fans, shaded windows which do not allow direct sunlight to fall on books or readers, and similar traditional practices, are far more effective protectors of the collection than hermetically sealed buildings in which the temperature and humidity will rise almost uncontrollably if the environmental control systems fail.

There is no reason why any library should be dirty; the regular cleaning of books and shelves is a basic procedure in any preservation programme. Windows can be shaded, and, where necessary, screened against flying insects when they are open. Both the level and the sources of artificial light can be regulated. Fitting ultraviolet filters to existing lights is cheap and easy; ensuring that the level of light is no more than is necessary for comfortable working conditions is economically desirable, quite apart from any other consideration.

EMERGENCIES AND DISASTERS

Everything a library does, involves risk of one sort or another. But there are levels of risk. Librarians continually deal with crises and emergencies of various types, but the term is often used so loosely as to weaken the true meaning of the term 'emergency'. Budget cuts, censorship efforts, and sudden threats from difficult patrons may be among the day-to-day challenges of operating a publicly supported, highly visible, heavily used service in a building generally open to the public, but these are not the types of emergencies in which lives or property are immediately threatened.

Emergencies are situations that arise suddenly and need immediate reaction. By their very nature, emergencies are sudden, so you don't have a lot of time to think things through at the moment they occur. Maybe that is why they're called emergencies; if they came with fair warning, reasoned and effective responses would be easier to formulate and effect. Libraries are not immune to emergencies, crises, and disasters, although such incidents are thankfully rare.

Different categories of disasters require correspondingly different responses. For definitional purposes, natural disasters are those caused by environmental phenomena, while human disasters are those resulting from human activity, both intentional and unintentional, malevolent and careless.

Still, many library administrators fail to acknowledge, understand, or plan for the biggest, most costly, and most serious crises of all: emergencies or disasters that could shut down libraries for weeks, months, or even forever. Having an Emergency Preparedness Plan (EPP) in place before an emergency situation develops allows you to plan and to make decisions about emergency response and recovery. When disaster strikes, the actions taken in the first minutes or hours can mean a vast difference to the health and safety of staff and patrons. Prompt reaction will also have a positive effect on how much of the library's collection, equipment, and facilities can be salvaged, and how soon normal operations can be resumed.

All hazard insurance in force is a must, but frequently insurance does not fully cover the cost of disasters and emergencies. The costs of property damage and business interruption can normally be offset by adequate insurance, but uninsured losses can also occur, such as loss of employees; cost of temporary equipment and facilities for use during recovery; increased insurance premium costs; and increased costs following recovery and restoration. An EPP consists of the development, documentation, testing, evaluation, and implementation of policies, procedures, organisational structure, information, and resources that a library can use to assess potential hazards and develop and prepare appropriate responses to those hazards and strategies for recovery.

While EPP objectives may differ substantially from one library to another, they should always be directed toward the protection of people, protection of property, and preparation for the library to resume normal services as soon as possible. Each library has special needs that must be fully addressed within its own EPP. Review your facilities, staff, services, products, and processes carefully to create the best EPP for your library. Creating a comprehensive EPP for your library's specific situation may seem at first to be an overwhelming task.

However, according to many insurance underwriters, an EPP is nothing more than a series of documents, tasks, teams, and processes. The message is clear and to the point: Don't underestimate the possibility that disaster could strike your library at any time. Be prepared. Start developing an EPP today. It is, however, probably unlikely that your library need start from scratch in developing its plan. Borrowing liberally from successful emergency planning documents from other libraries—or from other agencies that experience similar conditions and problems—is normally not only permitted but is encouraged. There are few proprietary or protected aspects of emergency planning, and most agencies are more than happy to share their plans with others.

The term 'disaster management' merely emphasises the need for planning to safeguard people, equipment, materials, and all information created electronically or manually. The literature of disaster planning generally sets out the three salient principles of comprehensive planning and considers the impact of disasters on human beings and their mental and physical health. Experts agree that there is still much to be learned about planning for quick and effective recovery from disaster.

Since there are so many things that may threaten your library, you have a compelling need for an all-hazards emergency management programme. Such a plan is recommended for libraries of all sizes and types. Libraries need to have policies in force that cover all situations. The purpose of a library's Emergency Operating Plan (EOP) is to provide a legal framework for the management of emergencies and to give guidance for what to do when an emergency strikes. A well-crafted plan sets out actions in priority order for response to major emergencies involving catastrophic risk, injury, or damage to library personnel, the general public, or library property. The plan should clearly designate who is to do what when an emergency strikes and each staff member's responsibilities in the process of reaction and subsequent recovery.

When an emergency breaks out, library staff should be trained to do the following:

a) Know when to call, when to notify security, and when they, themselves, should act to respond to the crisis.
b) Quickly respond to each serious situation of illegal, violent, abusive, or threatening behaviour to take reasonable actions to protect life first, and then property and facilities.
c) Provide immediate first-aid medical care to injured persons where required.
d) Physically segregate and detain any person or persons committing the act and call for police assistance as required.
e) Report, keep evidence, and interview those involved.

When the all-clear has sounded and things regain a general semblance of normalcy, the library administration, together with the LSO, should consult with crisis management repre-sentatives of local or state government to determine actions to take to prevent these situations from occurring again. Since many emergencies are much publicised and result in large numbers of human casualties, it makes sense for libraries to attempt to identify risks beforehand, and to work out viable strategies for minimum confusion and maximum protection against hazards.

Library patrons have a right to expect library staff to seek to prevent, to respond to, and to manage emergencies effectively, together with assistance from law enforcement agencies, fire control facilities, and civil defence authorities. The library's responsibility for preventing emergencies and handling them smoothly when they do occur includes a number of components:

a) The library should do all it can to prevent, reduce, and mitigate the risk of an emergency situation occurring.
b) If the library is unable to prevent the emergency, it should do everything possible to reduce the severity of the consequences of such an event.
c) The director is responsible for all operations of the library and should thus be intimately involved in planning for and handling emergency situations.
d) A previously appointed Library Security Officer (LSO), chosen from full-time staff and trained in emergency management, should coordinate all library responses to emergencies.
e) The library's chain of command should clearly spell out the names and positions of those to whom each staff member reports and the names and telephone numbers of persons to call in the event of an emergency.
f) Background information regarding potential problems should be assembled and compiled into an Emergency Procedures Manual made available to all staff. Librarians

should find it easy to search out and gather such information, which is widely available from many sources.

g) Employee involvement and practice can best be effected by periodic drills of simulated emergencies, followed by troubleshooting critiques, discussions of procedures, and identification of steps to be taken in times of emergency.

h) Information about equipment, communication, first-aid, and safety needs should be discussed with all staff members in periodic workshops. Everyone working in the building should know the location and operation of such items of equipment as fire hoses, first-aid kits, emergency telephones, fire alarms, and smoke detectors.

i) Instruction on tactical strategies to be employed during an emergency should be conveyed to all staff in in-service training sessions and by memorandum and should also be part of the orientation procedures for all new staff members.

j) Coordination of effort with local police, firefighters, the Red Cross, and other members of the law enforcement and medical communities is helpful and sometimes essential.

Natural Disasters

Naturally, there is bound to be some overlap (e.g., such pairs as fire and structural damage, hurricane and flood). For each emergency situation, a list of precautions is provided that can minimise loss or damage to library buildings and collections. Emphasis is on practical disaster prevention for library buildings and materials, building maintenance, materials storage, and fire and arson. Mention is also made of preventive measures (alarm systems, interior protection), salvage efforts (restoration of the collection), and the library's physical plant and facility.

Earthquakes

Reduction of loss of life and property in earthquakes is a major goal of libraries in areas where earthquakes are known to occur. One way of minimising personal injury and property loss or damage from earthquakes and related phenomena is strict adherence to the state's or community's building code. A proper code will reduce chances of such hazards as structural collapse, water damage to library contents, and the spreading of fires. Such codes, naturally enough, vary considerably from region to region.

In Florida and coastal Louisiana, for example, the major problem is the threat of hurricanes and resultant wind and flood damage. Tornadoes have been reported in every state in the continental United States but tend to group around the nation's midsection. While earthquakes may be of little concern to East Coast states, preparation for that eventuality should be a serious concern for builders and maintainers of library buildings in western states.

Preventive steps might include any or all of the following measures:

a) Construction of earthquake-resistant library buildings, especially in areas of high seismic risk. Preventing structural collapse is especially desirable.
b) Coordination of information about seismic risk with land-use policy decisions and building activity.
c) Development of improved methods for controlling risks from earthquakes and planning for reconstruction and redevelopment after an earthquake.
d) Education and training of all library staff in earthquake procedures, with two goals: saving lives and avoiding panic.
e) Comprehensive earthquake insurance, covering replacement costs of materials equipment and structure
f) Building to the specifications and standards of the local or state code.
g) Regular and thorough inspections of the structural integrity of the library building, with recommended repairs and strengthening performed immediately.

h) Full compliance with code provisions.
i) Strict enforcement of the code, with stiff penalties for noncompliance or failure to correct problems in a reasonable length of time.

Significance of adequate insurance coverage for the buildings and contents of libraries cannot be exaggerated or overstressed. Previous lack of recognition of the need for protective and preventive measures against the threat of earthquakes has resulted in additional tragedy for too many libraries.

Volcanoes

Results of volcanic eruptions are devastating for human life and property alike. Lava, poison gases, associated earthquakes and other seismic activity, hurricane-force winds, tidal waves, and wind-borne showers of ash are all problems associated with volcanic activity, and all are dangerous to libraries, their occupants, and their collections. It is no coincidence that few libraries are menaced by lava flow during volcanic eruptions; no sensible building plan would recommend building in any proximity to an active volcano.

The eruption of Mount St. Helens serves as an example of how even planning and preparedness augmented by the latest technology cannot protect life or property against the fury of exploding volcanoes. Hazard assessment, while not able to prevent eruptions or earthquakes, can go a long way toward heightening awareness of vulnerability and helping plan responses to various problem situations. Since no library can get out of the path of flowing lava, no matter how slowly its course flows, the library must take sensible steps to safeguard its building and contents when other problems arise. In anticipation of an eruption, the library should research the best way to remove the deposited ash before it becomes a hazard and anticipate any health consequences for those responsible for getting rid of it.

Hurricanes and tornadoes

Hurricanes and tornadoes can affect libraries with powerful winds, devasting flooding, and tremendous loss of structure, contents and even loss of life. Hurricanes can devastate entire states as they come ashore. Even though hurricanes move slowly and so permit authorities to take steps to minimise hazards to human life, there is no way to get buildings out of their path. Given that a library cannot take evasive action, there are still things that can be done to minimise the damage.

The amount of damage sustainable by a library in the path of a hurricane, tornado, or windstorm is often a question of building codes. By code, library buildings in high-risk areas should have hardened and reinforced structural components and be elevated out of floodplains. Shatter-resistant windows and doors will help control interior damage. Self-contained power sources and insulated wiring also help. Evacuation procedures are of great importance, and should be practised before the storm strikes so that staff will be prepared and calm when an actual emergency hits.

A tornado is the most violent storm nature produces, and, in addition, its existence and course are the hardest to predict. The library is not afforded the luxury of days to batten down the hatches in anticipation of a tornado, but it should have some means of minimising such things as falling trees, shattered windows, and breached doors. Every community has a disaster preparedness person who should be invited to do a building audit to assist library staff in locating the most advantageous part of the building for safe shelter in the event of a tornado.

Flood and water damage

Flooding is generally conceded to be the most destructive and costly natural disaster faced. Flash floods result from torrential rain and may cause water damage in libraries, but most are accompanied by related problems like mud and debris, snakes, and, later, damaged, mildewed, and otherwise useless books and other materials, if prompt and effective measures are not taken to minimise loss. The unfortunate part is that such remedial methods of book recovery are extremely cost- and labour-intensive.

To save water-damaged books or those damaged during fire fighting operations, freeze them as quickly as practicable to prevent mildew, then dry them in a thermal vacuum chamber, thus restoring them to usable condition, even though a slight tang of smoke may be extremely hard to get rid of. A less expensive means of attempting to salvage water-damaged materials is air-drying them with fans continually in operation. In the aftermath of flood, a disaster team should be appointed from among existing staff, with the library security officer as its director and leader, and charged with immediate recovery of as many items as can be saved.

Fire

Libraries, especially because of the kinds of materials they contain, are far from fireproof, even if their walls and floors are made of materials that cannot burn. Fire prevention is everyone's business, and prudent precautions can reduce the numbers of accidental fires greatly. Reasons for the commission of library arson vary:

a) Arson fires may be set for the intended economic gain of an owner of a nearby building and the flames may spread to the library.

b) Fires may be set for the economic gain of the arsonist who receives payment for the deed.

c) Arson may also be a form of concealment of some other criminal act.

d) The object of setting the fire is sometimes personal satisfaction and gratification.

e) The fire may be set as revenge for wrongs, real or perceived.

f) Rarely but still occasionally, arson is committed in furtherance of —or publicity for—a political or social cause. A tip-off is when someone telephones a message from a group taking 'credit' for the blaze.

Dealing with fires from a library standpoint demands a two-pronged attack. Fires may be divided for convenience of discussion into two classes: external and internal. Internal fires occur within the building and to property therein. External fires, often accompanied by strong winds, can threaten buildings with total destruction.

As there is nothing the library can do to get the building out of harm's way, the best that can be hoped for is to minimise structural damage to the outside of the building, while protecting the building's contents and occupants to the extent possible. Multilevel libraries can be difficult for good response to fire. A loss of electricity often occurs when fire strikes. This severely limits lighting, and shuts down elevators and computer access, while creating confusion in building occupants and sometimes disabling alarm systems. Building evacuation is, of course, a primary concern, and all persons not required to maintain communications or to assist in evacuation should be removed immediately from the structure and relocated to places of safety.

Fire stairs should be used to conduct all persons out of the building in an orderly manner within five minutes of the initial alarm, with great care being taken to avoid panic. Once outside, there will be considerable milling about, with evacuees wondering what has happened and when they can re-enter the building, but staff may be of help in keeping patrons who elect to remain in the area well back from firefighters and their work.

Steps to be followed in the event of fire include the following:

a) Test alarm systems, smoke detectors, and fire extinguishers regularly.

b) Always report the alarm or actual fire to firefighters and police first before you are distracted or preoccupied.

c) Ensure that everyone takes fire alarms and fire drills seriously as though their lives depended on them, because they do. Even alarms that turn out to be false require full mobilisation.

d) Sound alarms immediately. Supplement or replace mechanical alarms by shouting a stern but carefully worded warning throughout the building. Direct everyone to leave the building with no exceptions permitted.

e) When the alarm sounds, make sure that everyone evacuates the building to a place of safety, no matter what the weather is like outside or what they're doing at the time.

f) Regularly inspect fire exits, ensure that signs are present and illuminated, and post diagrams showing the public the location of all emergency exits. Keep windows and doors closed and unlocked when evacuating the building.

g) Alert emergency, security, and operations staff who should be prepared in advance concerning evacuation procedures and policies. Prepare institution staff to evacuate themselves. Evacuate the public calmly.

h) Respond to the scene of a small fire with extinguishers.

i) Check security at all exits.

The most serious danger from fire is human injury or even loss of life. The loss of property should also be considered. Most library equipment is insured, but salvage operations should begin immediately. Electronic equipment protected by surge suppressors may not be harmed by lack of electricity. In the immediate aftermath of a major fire, all attention should be directed toward damage assessment and quick elimination of smoke. At least one security officer should be stationed as a round-the-clock security guard, to prevent looting or access by the merely curious who could be hurt by damaged building contents subsequent to fire.

As soon as practicable, library staff and any volunteers who may come forward should carefully begin picking up the pieces, sorting through the building contents, and doing a form of triage by choosing what needs attention first. Electrical systems, elevators, and fire alarms should be restored first. Exhaust and ventilation fans should be placed in as many sites as possible around the building to remove the lingering odour of smoke, and should be in operation 24 hours a day until the air is comfortably breathable.

In the aftermath of fire, a safety assessment of all structural components should be performed as soon as possible, after which the library should begin cleaning up with a view to reopening as soon as practical. The clean-up operation should begin with salvage operations on damaged books and other materials, followed by cleaning and scrubbing surface dirt and soot from walls and ceilings, carpet shampooing and deodorising, and upholstery and curtain cleaning.

Manmade Disasters

Libraries, whatever you may wish them to be or think they ought to be, are not always tranquil havens of serenity where one can lose oneself in thought, study, contemplation, and peace. They are also workplaces, and, as such, they are vulnerable to a growing concern of people everywhere: workplace violence. Every library, regardless of size and whether it has a large security force, a small one, or none at all, should consider the merits of forming a violence response team to cope with outbreaks of violence in the library building.

The potential for violent behaviour on the part of any person is difficult to predict, and relying on a stereotypical image of what the violence-prone person looks like or will do can be extremely hazardous. That's why the library should have a violence response team in place before problems occur, prepared to respond quickly, gather facts about a potentially explosive incident, and decide whether to intervene, call the police, or take some other form of action. Prior to forming such a team, the library management should conduct an initial risk assessment. Beyond that, all staff should be trained to report any threat of violence immediately.

Individual judgement may be required to determine whether a given incident requires a response. Such judgements should be based on clues such as use of certain words, body language, and tone of voice, and not merely on appearance, hygiene, prejudice, or instincts. As the LSO or staff member in charge, your first job is to defuse the problematic individual's level of stress and anger by remaining calm and deliberate, not responding to anger in kind, and speaking soothingly while help is being summoned. Remember that you are responsible for the lives and safety of everyone in the building, which should dissuade you from doing anything sudden, precipitous, or heroic to solve the problem or end the confrontation. Actually, the best idea is probably to call the police at the first threat of violence.

Bomb threats

Terrorists normally choose high-profile places for their bombings because they hope to create the maximum disruption possible and receive the greatest amount of publicity. New York's World Trade Centre and Oklahoma City's Federal Building are two chilling examples. In this sense, libraries are fortunate in not being high-profile public buildings, but while libraries are far down the list of sites chosen by terrorist bombers, bomb threats are being phoned into libraries with increasing frequency. Since so many people enter libraries each day, each bomb threat must be taken seriously as a hazard to life, limb, and property, and all staff members should be acquainted with procedures for handling them when they occur.

Not all bomb threats need result in an evacuation, although prudent library officers usually authorise evacuation of the building because there is no way to tell. Since cultural institutions tend to have good reputations, they are rarely the target of serious bomb attempts. But warped or fanatical minds may not distinguish between good and bad institutions, and deranged persons interested in running up a body count may find them ideal targets of opportunity.

Recovery procedures

Emergency recovery procedures in libraries when a disaster occurs may include measures such as freezing and freeze-drying of waterlogged materials as alternatives to just declaring books a loss and space-drying of rooms damaged. In the aftermath of any emergency, library officials should perform impromptu triage to figure out what can't wait for attention, what can, and what can get along without any immediate consideration. In the absence of immediate insurance funding, triage will dictate what needs to be done first to get the library ready for a speedy reopening.

Based on the assessment of the damage, proposed repairs, and temporary services available, the library administrator or LSO should communicate with the library's community of users, outlining the situation and projecting the restoration of services. The LSO should communicate with all department heads, explaining the scope of the problem, what is being done to fix the damage, and an estimate of the time required for reopening with business as usual.

Public information addressing the concerns of patrons who have borrowed materials and want to know when and where to return them may help to forestall the calls and questions likely to arise. One option, should the circulation desk be closed to the public, is that returns can be continued through the book drops or outside collection boxes. If the building is declared unsafe or unusable after the emergency, a temporary 'home' for the library may be established to take care of library services such as reference, circulation, and inter-library loan.

Carpets and curtains may make a library attractive and homey, and help reduce noise in public rooms and heat and sun damage in open spaces, yet the libraries easiest to return to normal have no carpeting or curtains at all. Still, modern libraries have found carpeting and curtains to be both aesthetic and useful in sound suppression. Therefore, every effort should be made to protect carpet during the recovery phase by taping down sheets of plastic in aisles and walkways. Even so, soot from burned equipment and materials may well spread to furniture, walls, and carpeting just from being kicked up by the feet of the rescuers and others.

The object of all these efforts is to get the library ready to reopen to the public as soon as possible, consistent with the safety and comfort of all who enter the building. There's a trade-off at work here: You can have your library back quickly, or you can have it clean—even cleaner than it was before the emergency—but you shouldn't realistically expect to have both at the same time. Money, too, is a factor in the aftermath of emergencies. Once you find out how much is available to commit to recovery activities and how soon funds can be encumbered for the jobs that need to be done, you may be able to project more accurately and realistically the library's date of reopening or restoration of full services.

Most patrons will accept with good cheer less-than-ideal conditions, as, for example, when the main layer of soot has been cleaned or removed, but considerable mess still remains in the building. A few are bound to complain, but a few are always going to complain. The majority of library users will generally be pleased to have access, however, and will gladly overlook or forgive the mess and cooperate by working around those areas. Cleaning and repainting of scorched or mud-encrusted walls, also a disruption to normal library function, will help greatly with restoring an acceptable level of visual and olfactory tolerance.

Fire alarm systems may have to be completely restored and tested before the building can be reopened to the public. Patrons and staff alike will experience a certain amount of inconvenience in the aftermath of a disaster, but signs posted in prominent places that demonstrate awareness of problems help considerably in keeping the public informed, if not necessarily delighted with the speed of recovery.

PRESERVATION OF DATA

Historians have increasingly recognised the value of newspapers as historical sources, while modern methods of indexing have made possible the more effective retrieval of the huge quantities of information which they contain. Demand for them by users of research collections, and especially of historical collections, is consequently increasing.

The preservation of newspapers presents two related physical problems: there are huge numbers of them, and they are generally printed on very poor paper. It is these two factors which have determined the direction of newspaper preservation in recent years. The sheer scale of the problem made it inevitable that newspapers would be among the first groups of material to be the subject of mass microfilming programmes for preservation purposes. Indeed, there was a secondary advantage, in addition to the need to transfer the information to a more durable medium.

Few libraries hold complete runs of early newspapers, and the preservation microfilms, by drawing on the resources of a number of institutions, were more complete than the holdings of any individual library. Needless to say, large-scale microfilming of newspapers calls for large-scale capital investment. This has been a serious obstacle to more projects being undertaken, despite the fact that such projects are generally considered to be desirable. It should be added, however, that there is sufficient demand for newspapers for the films to be a viable commercial proposition.

A considerable number of newspapers have been filmed either by commercial firms, or in collaborative ventures between companies and libraries. There are some generally accepted requirements which are specific to the filming of newspapers. These include the making of minor repairs before filming, so that crumpled and folded pages, for example, are opened out and flattened, and missing issues are checked and noted. This is in addition to such normal practices as ensuring that materials are carefully handled, leader film is provided, the reduction ratio is clearly stated, and the end-product is checked against the original before any copies are made from the master negative.

Local and regional newspapers are often found in the public library in their place of publication and sometimes nowhere else. Similarly, incomplete runs in major libraries may be supplemented by copies found in local collections in libraries, record offices and even the newspaper offices themselves. The need to know where newspapers are to be found, and to ensure that archival copies are indeed of an archival standard, is a matter of concern to everyone involved, and is an issue which could arise in any public library or county record office. The second category of material which helps to exemplify some of the practical questions involved in preservation management is periodicals, and in particular the learned and scientific journals to be found in academic libraries.

Journals

Journals of all types are of heavy use, and perhaps to the maximum, or only, use which they are ever likely to have. The traditional approach to this problem was to regard the most heavily used materials as the priorities for binding, and to ensure that they were bound as quickly as possible after the publication of the volume was complete. This is successful enough in the context of a specialised scientific collection, although it may not be more generally applicable. There is, however, an alternative point of view. If a volume of a journal of immediate, but comparatively short-term, interest is sent away for binding as soon as it is completed by the publication of its final part, that part will be unavailable to users during precisely the period of time when it is in heaviest demand. In science, medicine and engineering this point is particularly relevant.

From the user's standpoint, the availability of unbound parts is far more important than their long-term preservation. This is a perfectly legitimate view, and save in research libraries seeking to retain long runs for permanent reference, it need not be a matter of too great concern. Deciding what materials to send for binding, and the order of priority, will ultimately be a question which is answered in relation to use and resources. The greater the number of issues per volume, the higher the priority for binding when the publication of the volume is complete. This is partly dictated by publishing conventions, since the more frequent publications tend to be in larger formats which are less easy to store satisfactorily when they are unbound. It is significant, however, that newsletters and letter journals also appear at monthly or even more frequent intervals; these are often of comparatively ephemeral interest at least as far as heavy use is concerned. By contrast, the classic four-part-per-year journal is typically in octavo format, and can be stored in open-topped pamphlet boxes, or, indeed, directly on the shelf.

Paperbacks

In recent years, public libraries, in particular, have purchased paperbacks in large quantities for two reasons. First, it is felt that they are more attractive to some of the less enthusiastic users of the library, and especially perhaps to children, to whom they are more familiar that the superficially more serious hardback. Secondly, they are of course cheaper. It is the latter factor which is the more important factor for our purposes. If the paperback rather than the hardback edition of a title is selected, this may have several consequences. It may allow more copies of a popular title to be bought, or it may allow more titles to be bought than would otherwise be possible.

In times of serious financial restraint, it may even be the only way to maintain a reasonable level and breadth of purchases at all. Whatever the motive the object of the exercise is defeated if the lifespan of the paperback is so short that it has to be replaced, so incurring additional costs, or it is necessary to withdraw it while the title is still in demand. Some criteria which might be applied to the selection and protection of paperbacks.

In general, an 'untreated' paperback, that is, a paperback as issued by its publisher, was found to remain in a usable condition for about one year of library use. For popular fiction this would seem to be adequate. The additional expense involved in inserting the books in protective plastic jackets did not significantly improve the situation. Simple reinforcement also had a minimal effect. Only a full case-binding really extended the lifespan of the book, and even that presented some difficulties. The study was primarily concerned with comparing the properties of various binding styles, and did not really take cost factors into account, although they were, of course, implicit.

For the collection manager, however, they are an explicit and crucially important consideration. A typical paperback novel sells at about £2.00, or about 25 per cent of the price of the hardback. Binding may almost double the real cost of the book before it reaches the shelves. In other words, two untreated copies can be replaced in twelve months' time, or four copies can be provided immediately to meet demand, for the same price as one strengthened copy which still has to be replaced at about the same time. Strengthening the binding to make an appreciable difference to its durability may raise the cost to near to the hardback price, and since even a bound paperback never seems to achieve the strength of a hardback, it is probably desirable to buy the hardback in the first place. A fourth and final issue which illuminates some general points is that of the transfer of materials to more protected storage.

RESTORATION

Most of the library items may only need a minimal amount of repair, such as mending simple tears, tipping in loose pages, recasting, cleaning, etc. Care must be taken not to overtreat, as incorrectly applied repairs may cause serious problems in rebinding or preservation at a later date. In-house repair units may also be capable of rebinding, including resewing, making new cases, etc. Smaller libraries may have to send such materials to a commercial binder. Some categories of materials will probably be sent to commercial binders by larger libraries because of volume, lack of equipment, or trained personnel to adequately rebind in house.

The processes that may be carried on in an in-house binding and repair unit of a library are given below:

i) *Mending*: Restoration, not involving replacement with any new material or the separation of book from cover.

ii) *Repairing*: Partial rehabilitation of a worn volume, the amount of work done being less than the minimum involved in rebinding and more than the maximum involved in mending.

iii) *Reinforcing*: Strengthening the structure of a weakened volume, usually by adding material.

iv) *Recasting*: Replacing the cover on a volume which has come out of its cover or has loosened in its cover, the sewing and cover being still in good condition.

v) *Rebacking*: Attaching a new shelf back on a volume without any other binding.

vi) *Re-covering*: The process of making a new cover and of attaching it to the volume.

vii) *Re-sewing*: The process of taking the volume out of its cover, removing the old sewing, sewing anew, and replacing in the same cover.

De-acidification

Deacidification is the process of reducing the acidity of paper to a neutral or alkaline state. A number of methods are effective, but they can only arrest continued deterioration of acid, not restore paper to its original state. Barrow developed a method in the 1940s that involved bathing the paper first in a solution of calcium hydroxide to neutralise the acid, followed by bathing it in calcium bicarbonate to add buffering agents. A later method was developed using magnesium bicarbonate which both neutralised the acid and alkalised the paper. The principal drawback to aqueous methods for de-acidification of books is the necessity to disbind, treat one sheet at a time, and follow by drying, resewing, and rebinding.

There may also be problems with inks, fragility of paper, etc. These processes should be undertaken only by trained conservators conversant with the chemistry and techniques involved and having a thorough knowledge of the materials to be treated. A number of non-aqueous processes have been developed, but most have not had widespread adoption because of toxicity or the flammability of the chemicals used.

Mass de-acidification is necessary to preserve our deteriorating collections, as the cost of de-acidification of single items is prohibitive unless an item is of sufficient rarity to justify such an expenditure. Mass de-acidification experiments have been undertaken by both the Library of Congress and the Canadian National Archives. The process that seems to hold the most promise is mass de-acidification with diethyl zinc.

Williams and Kelly report their research and state that vapour phase neutralisation and buffering must include the following elements:

i) The paper must be uniformly neutralised.
ii) The paper should be buffered as close to pH7 as possible, on the alkaline side. Higher pH changes the colour or tint of inks and art work and yellows paper which contains groundwood.
iii) The paper should be given an alkaline reserve equivalent to three per cent calcium carbonate.
iv) The treatments must penetrate books and masses of books in a reasonable time.
v) The treatment, although applied as a gas, must not come back out of the paper. This implies that a reaction with cellulose takes place or that there is a polymerisation of gaseous material in the cellulose or that two gases react to make a non-volatile product *in situ,* etc.
vi) The treatment should not impart an odour to the paper.
vii) The treated paper should be non-toxic to humans.
viii) No new problems should be introduced by the treatment such as darkening of the paper, damage to the leather, etc.
ix) The treatment should be reasonable in cost.

De-accessioning

Weeding may be defined in terms of removal from the collection (de-accession) through transferring titles to a storage facility, replacement in a microformat, or complete withdrawal. Evans cites three reasons for weeding a collection: (i) to save space, (ii) to improve access, and (iii) to save money.

A well-planned weeding programme is essential to a professionally managed collection. Many factors will determine the programme to be developed, including the purpose of the library and clientele served. A small public library whose clientele is interested in the latest information and editions, and with limited space, will develop a much different programme than a large research library whose purpose may be to collect in depth a wide variety of research materials in many areas. Space is most likely to be one major determining factor that will force weeding, as most libraries cannot indefinitely provide new facilities for shelving.

Compact storage may be a temporary solution; converting to microforms may also be a solution in some instances to solve shelving needs. Organising a weeding programme is not an easy task, and unless weeding is given some priority, it is often an area of collection management that is overlooked in many libraries. Some view the removal of any book from the collection as a sacrilegious practice, but practicality dictates the need for management of the collection through a well-developed weeding programme.

There is a wide divergence of opinion on the type of weeding programmes that may be best; a study of the purpose and use of the collection (both current and projected) will help dictate the weeding programme to be implemented. In a public library in which browsing is important, the titles most circulated should be on the shelves. In a research library or a closed stack collection, shelving the most highly circulated materials together may not be an important factor.

Many associations and organisations have issued standards for weeding, but they are uneven and quickly outdated. Many book selection or collection development statements of individual libraries contain weeding statements that when applied can be useful to other libraries establishing a weeding programme.

One of the most often used criteria for weeding is the circulation record of a title. If the library wishes the most used titles readily accessible, circulation is an excellent standard. A method must be developed to determine the amount of time a title remains on the shelf uncirculated and projection of any future circulation. If the title is to be stored rather than deaccessioned, the problem is not as great because an item in storage could be brought back into the core circulating system.

An informative study by Slote suggests that circulation patterns for fiction in public libraries can be used to identify core collections. Fussler and Simon in their study recommended a combination of factors in determining titles to be weeded, including date of publication, language, and circulation history.

Treuswell's measures and criteria for weeding based on circulation have generated much interest since their publication; Treuswell's techniques are either attacked or proclaimed as outstanding criteria for weeding. Turner presents a review of the Treuswell method that uses calculations based on the amount of time elapsed since the last circulation.

Age has been suggested as a criterion for weeding, but it must be very carefully applied, along with other factors. Age might be employed as a factor in the selection for storage, but even here potential use and circulation must be considered. Muller in her study indicated that age is a poor predictor of future or even current use. The criteria for monographs and serials will also be varied. Age as a factor can be applied to obsolete material that may be superseded by later works or subsequent editions if the historical need is not a factor.

There will also be a wide variance in subjects; for example, between science and the humanities, and even between scientific subjects such as chemistry and mathematics or medicine and botany. Slote, in a review of the literature on weeding, concludes that the age of the volume was found to be somewhat predictive of future use, but generally of little practical value.

Storage

In selecting a storage facility, whether rental or new construction, all pertinent problems must be carefully reviewed in terms of the goals and services to be provided. Cooperative storage centres may be a solution for some libraries. In a storage facility, compact shelving of some type will generally be used. Traditional shelving practices are inefficient in the use of floor space, whereas compacting may increase the capacity of books stored in an area up to 100 per cent. An increase in the number of books stored can be achieved by shelving according to size, decreasing aisle widths, as well as the installation of mechanised systems that move along rails in order to provide access.

Fussler and Simon and Trueswell suggest mechanised guidelines for selection of materials for storage. Other writers have developed similar models, but there is no general agreement on the best method. Using circulation data is most often suggested; that is, those books that have not circulated in the most recent five years would be the most likely candidates for placement into storage. Circulation, coupled with other data such as date of publication, language, subject, etc., should also be considered. Serials and monographs differ in use, and different criteria should be applied. It is more costly to select monographs for storage than larger runs of serial titles and large monograph sets. Each library must carefully plan a programme to build a storage selection programme to best meet the needs of the library in terms of space and service to its patrons, just as it would develop a selection programme for new acquisitions.

There are no standard or established criteria for the selection of storage space. Space may become available in an existing building by rearrangement of space or the instalation of compact shelving. Some libraries have constructed storage facilities adjacent to or distant from central buildings. Such decisions to establish a storage facility are based on many factors, including the cost and availability of space, cost of transporting materials between more distant locations, etc. As an alternative to a new building, some libraries have leased storage facilities. The cost of such facilities may be a major factor, but leasing is an alternative to large expenditures for a new building, an annex, or a separate storage facility.

As library networks have been established in recent years, there has been some movement toward establishing cooperative storage centers, but most efforts to date have centered on union lists, shared or cooperative acquisitions, cooperative processing, and open access to patrons, especially students and faculties of cooperating colleges and universities.

Almost all libraries will collect some microforms in the selection and acquisition processes. The amount of material available in microformat has increased year by year since the 1940s. In order to build research collections of retrospective serials, newspapers, and rare books, there is often no other practical alternative than to purchase in microform. Converting paper copy in existing collections presents other problems, and each library must study its needs and the specific costs relating to such conversion.

Handling of Books

Proper handling of books is one of the most important factors in their preservation. Bindings can be readily broken and pages and spines torn, if not carefully handled. Shelving staff should be instructed as to proper handling. Books should not be placed on their fore edges as this will weaken bindings. Book drops for return of circulating books should be designed to avoid damage as books are deposited and should be emptied regularly to prevent overcrowding.

Cleanliness is important, as dirt on shelves can cause abrasion and staining of covers and pages. Cleaning schedules, including vacuuming and dusting, should be established. If all areas are not regularly cleaned and refuse is not removed, problems with vermin may occur. New acquisitions, if necessary, should be cleaned before being placed on shelves as well as the shelves themselves. Apart from the aesthetic factors, cleanliness is important in maintaining library collections in good condition.

Improper display techniques can damage library materials in many of the same ways as improper handling. Unsupported books lying open and flat may have bindings broken or damaged due to stress. Display cradles should always be used if possible. Cunha states, "display cases should have protective glass that absorbs both heat and damaging radiation," and also that illumination should be from the outside or "concealed fluorescent lamps that are screened by plastic ultraviolet filters." For extended exhibits, pages should be turned periodically to avoid fading. Temperature and humidity inside a display case can become a hostile environment and should be controlled to avoid damage. Descriptions on cards or paper should be checked for acidity before being placed on covers or pages.

PRESERVATION PROGRAMMES

The role of the manager is essentially in the determination of policy and its supervision, a role which requires a knowledge of the preservation field, without implying any need to acquire technical skills. This point has often been made, and is now widely accepted in professional circles. Perhaps the one group of exceptions is to be found among some of the more traditional rare book librarians who still seem to regard detailed technical knowledge and even some benchwork skills as an essential part of the librarian's armoury, a view shared to a limited extent by a few educators. If we leave aside the question of benchwork skills, there are three areas of administrative activity to be considered:

i) the organisation of the bindery and other workshops.

ii) the determination of the work to be undertaken and the styles and techniques to be employed.

iii) the role of all library staff in ensuring that materials are handled and used in a way which is consistent with their optimal survival.

The first stage of administartion of peservation in libraries is to determine whether it is appropriate to have in-house facilities at all. Most of the libraries which had in-house facilities also used external binderies when it was considered appropriate. The normal pattern seems to be to use commercial binderies for standard work, such as periodical binding, while undertaking more complex operations in-house. In particular, many libraries prefer to use their own employees and facilities for the repair and conservation of older material, although the British Library has in recent years also used outside binderies for that purpose. Indeed, it has been forcefully argued that there are financial advantages in employing outside organisations or individuals even for high-level conservation work on rare books and manuscripts. There are savings in the indirect costs of employing staff, and it is suggested that the self-employed conservator, working for fees, is likely to maintain a higher rate of productivity than a salaried employee of a library or record office.

In-house facilities are expensive. Moreover, there is a limited supply of skilled persons to work in them, and the commercial binderies are, on the whole, able to offer higher wages than are libraries and record offices. It may be significant that a book by a distinguished preservation manager, intended as a guide to individuals and small libraries, says nothing about the establishment and administration of the bindery itself. It is, apparently assumed that any necessary work will be done elsewhere. The same considerations apply to other preservation facilities. Paper repair and other laboratory activities call for skills which are not widely available, while the facilities themselves occupy a good deal of space. There are legal requirements in relation to health and safety for the use and storage of chemicals and the use and maintenance of equipment. Traditionally, many record offices have indeed had in-house paper repair and conservation facilities, and continue to do so. In fact, the whole subject of conservation is rightly regarded as a crucial area of the archivist's professional activities and hence an essential part of his or her professional education.

Some research libraries have initiated paper-repair laboratories in recent years, especially for their manuscript collections. In general, however, few libraries will wish to move into this field. All libraries have some reprographic capacity, if only for photocopying. Most libraries with research collections also have more sophisticated facilities intended to provide transparencies, 35-min microfilm, bromide prints and the like, for users. These operations usually work on the expectation of breaking even, and in some cases as profit-making activities. Few in-house studios, however, can cope with large-scale microfilming programmes, although some libraries have established special facilities where surrogate creation has become a principal element in the preservation strategy. The British Library is one such institution but few libraries would feel able, financially or technically, to follow that example. Again the problem is one of workflow. Even for quite large-scale substitution programmes, the commercial microfilm bureau—or better still micropublishers whose sales will help to offset the cost of creating the master negatives and perhaps produce a royalty or fee for the library—are a distinctly preferable option.

Whether the work is undertaken in-house or externally, it will be library staff who determine what work is actually to be done. This decision-making process falls essentially into two stages. First, the material to be repaired has to be selected, a subject with which we have already dealt at some length. Secondly, the nature of the work to be undertaken has to be decided, and for this to be done effectively some technical knowledge is indeed essential, so that the librarian understands the options which are available.

Having decided in principle that a particular item or a particular class of material is to be preserved, the next stage is to decide whether preservation is to be in original format or in surrogate form. This decision is partly financial, although the nature of the material itself, and its condition, are also factors. Surrogate creation is, in general, very uneconomic for single items such as one book or a small group of documents.

The larger the number of uniform items, such as a run of a newspaper, the more economically attractive does surrogacy become, especially if there might be a spin off in the sale of copies of the microfilm to other libraries. It is not usual in Britain, although it is in some American libraries, to discard the originals once the master negative has been made. If the book is important enough to film, it is important enough to need more than mere neglect to preserve the original.

Microfilming preservation generally makes sense only when undertaken on a large scale for a large number of items; this is why a run of a newspaper is so ideal a candidate for such treatment. When programmes are undertaken cooperatively, or as joint ventures with publishers, the costs may be even more favourable to the library. The creation of surrogates is not always the most desirable solution to a preservation problem, even when it is technically feasible and economically viable.

Although there are large categories of material for which it is probably the most appropriate option, there will always be a large, and perhaps larger, number of cases in which it is not. In such cases, the choice is essentially between the repair of the damage or the replacement of the item. In many cases, the latter option is not available. Indeed, the scarcity of the item which is considered to be worth preserving will be one factor in determining the priority which it takes in the competition for resources and skills. In practice, one course of action, or rather inaction, is what has sometimes been called 'benign neglect', that is, storage in reasonably good conditions together with the enforcement of high standards of handling and use. For rarely used materials this has been a favoured option in some libraries in recent years, not least because it has the great merit of costing almost nothing.

More recently, however, the practice has been challenged from an authoritative source. Some active intervention is needed, this may take the form of repair of the paper, or, more frequently, of the binding. Paper repair is generally confined to rare and valuable materials, especially manuscripts and archival documents. The one exception is the mass deacidification of embrittled books, although, as we have seen, these processes are still at a comparatively early stage of development.

Most conservation work is, in practice, concerned with the repair or replacement of damaged or decayed bindings. Repair is usually cheaper, although it may not be possible for very badly damaged material. Where the book is of historical interest, and especially if the original binding is significant, it is always desirable to be as conservative as possible in undertaking repairs. It is often possible, for example, to reuse the original boards and their original leather covering, while using new leather for the spine and perhaps resewing the text-block.

Original endpapers have to be preserved if they bear, for example, book-plates, other marks of provenance or inscriptions of some kind. Indeed, such endpapers are bound in even if they are no longer functional as endpapers, in order to preserve the historical evidence which they offer. It is often more appropriate to reback, that is, to repair the existing binding, using as little new material as possible, than it is to rebind, that is to remove the remains of the existing binding, and to replace it with a completely new one. Rebacking and rebinding are not the only options for damaged books. For older books it may be deemed appropriate to use specially made boxes, and these have indeed become an important instrument of preservation in the last ten years. The 'phase' box is a made-to-measure box, constructed of acid-free or chemically inert card, designed to protect the book both on the shelf and in transit between the shelf and the reader's desk. It is made of a single piece of card, with a hinged lid, and sometimes with ties to ensure that the book cannot fall out when the box is removed from the shelf. Such boxes are comparatively cheap to make, costing as little as about £10 for one suitable for an eighteenth-century octavo of 200 or so pages.

Consequently, large numbers of books can be protected. Boxes may be used either where the book needs protection until the time comes for full-scale repairs or because for some reason it may be undesirable to resew or rebind, in order to preserve historical or bibliographical evidence. In practice, of course, these options apply largely to older books or books deemed to be of some permanent historical value. For current materials likely to be of comparatively limited or medium-term interest only, different considerations may apply. These have already been discussed in several contexts, including the issues which arise in considering the preservation of periodicals and paperbacks.

In every case, however, it is essential that the binder has clear instructions from the librarian. The binder will carry out such instructions, but cannot be expected to interpret them or to make deductions about them. It is certainly not the binder's business to guess at what they ought to have been when they are either absent or inadequate. For straightforward work, only straightforward instructions are required. These should specify the general nature of the work to be done, the materials to be used and any special requirements. Thus, for rebinding a recent book, the specification need be no more than 'library binding, blue cloth', together with a note of the words or other matter, if any, to be embossed on the spine.

For periodicals, the instructions are typically a little more complicated, since they have to specify how the parts are to be arranged, whether such material as covers, advertising pages and supplements are to be retained, and if so where they are to be bound in. The instructions will also specify what is to be done about the title-page, index and table of contents, as well as external matters such as the colour of cloth to be used and the wording to be used on the spine. The last two items will be standardised in most libraries, but they do differ from library to library.

Many libraries keep standard or specimen bindings in their own binderies which are then imitated year after year to maintain uniformity on the shelves. Commercial binderies have their own specimens, standards and exemplars from which the customer can choose, but they will also create and maintain a design to the customer's own specification. Instructions are normally sent to the bindery in writing, and often on proformas designed for the purpose. In some libraries, the binding records are now automated, and instructions therefore appear in the form of hardcopy print-out from the relevant file. Finally, when completed work is returned from the binder, at least a random sample is normally checked to ensure that the instructions have indeed been followed.

However, preservation is not a matter for specialists alone, or indeed only for professional librarians. It is the concern of all staff and all users of a library. A great deal can be achieved in a preservation programme by creating the conditions in which the rate of deterioration of materials is reduced to a minimum. This can, of course, be very expensive, if it is conceived in terms of environmental control systems, significant building modifications, and the like. It can be done very cheaply, however, by simple housekeeping measures which are an integral part of the administration of a well-run library. Junior staff are the key to success. It is they who handle books and deal with users. They can act both as the detectors of the first signs of damage or decay, and as the exemplars in the handling and care of materials.

Good housekeeping begins with the shelves. Ideally, these should be of metal, not wood, since metal is not susceptible to the biological hazards which can beset any organic substance. Metal is easier to keep clean, and less likely to be broken or damaged. The proper care of books on the shelves is the starting-point of a preservation programme. This means, among other things, regular and careful dusting using soft dusters and no chemical cleaning medium. Even in heavily used reference collections, most books spend most of their lives on the shelves. Junior staff have to be taught to keep the shelves tidy, and in particular to ensure that they are always tidy at the beginning of the day. This has the psychological effect on users of encouraging them to try to maintain that level of tidiness, whereas untidy shelves can only become worse as time goes on. A few simple rules also need to be applied by the professional staff in determining where and how books shall be stored.

Outsize books should be shelved upright in a separate sequence, not foredge down in normally spaced shelves. Very large volumes, such as atlases or bound volumes of newspapers, should be shelved flat, even in open-access areas. Special shelving, or other storage systems, is needed for maps and audiovisual materials. Current parts of periodicals may need protective covers as a temporary measure before they go for boxing or binding.

Pamphlets, again in a special sequence, are better stored in boxes than directly on the shelves. These are all simple matters of good practice, and are not beyond the realistic aspirations and capability of any library. Staff should be encouraged not to overload trolleys, not to carry too many books, not to pile books too high on desks and tables or on or behind counters. Trolleys are needed for books returned to the circulation desk before they go for sorting and shelving. The trolleys should also be kept tidy, and, when they are moved, moved carefully.

In all of these cases, exhortation is probably more effective than instruction, but it is also important that the professional staff make clear to juniors the extent and the limits of their authority in dealing with any recalcitrant users, and are then prepared to support them. Staff in general need to be made aware that preservation is an aspect of collection management; otherwise some of this may seem a little trivial or pedantic. Circulation staff should be empowered, and indeed required, to set aside books which are returned from loan in need of repair. This is not for the purpose of punishing a particular user who may or may not have been responsible for the damage. It is rather because a minor and cheap repair now may save the time and expense of a major repair later. A proper reporting system will be needed to ensure that any such suspicions reach the preservation manager, or other responsible professional, immediately. Building design, the internal layout of the building, and furnishings are also critical elements in preservation.

In research libraries, or in rare book rooms, it is essential that readers' tables are sufficiently generous in size to allow books to be used properly without piling them one on top of another. Where particularly valuable or fragile books and manuscripts are being used, table top lecterns are essential; plastic forceps to hold the page open without exerting too much pressure on it are a useful additional precaution. Some regulations are also necessary to ensure effective preservation. Apart from obvious rules about the use and misuse of books, it is normal to forbid the use of flat-platen photocopying machines with older books or manuscripts.

A library which wishes to create a preservation-conscious culture needs a senior member of staff responsible for it. In many, and perhaps most, libraries this is not a full-time job, and is perhaps most logically associated either with the post-holder responsible for collection management and development, or with the professional librarian with overall responsibility for the running of the building.

The essential function of preservation manager is that he or she has a general oversight of all the matters which we have been discussing, and is, therefore, in a position to have a policy level view of the library's preservation situation. He or she is the determiner of the policies and priorities which will in turn allow logical and consistent decisions to be made in individual cases.

7

Information Future of System

Libraries as a non-profit services industry developed their key product called information. To create a positive image, the library must demonstrate the marketing approach in such a way that it observes efficiency and effectiveness in LIS (Library Information System). Librarians and information professionals must harness marketing concepts and techniques to their other very considerable powers if their services are to survive and prosper.

Library managers may need to know the tacts and traits of marketing. Library and information centres that apply the marketing concept try to disseminate its services to satisfy users needs through predetermined and well defined, coordinated plans and activities. Therefore, marketing and its techniques, if applied to LIS, can help to fulfil the expected needs of information seekers. If the non-business organisations recognise their marketing roles, they will turn increasingly to the body of marketing principles worked out by business situations.

A library must emphasise the basic needs of customers to be served. The basic product of LIS are information, not the physical form of books, journals, electronic diskettes and so on. Library and information centres are such an organisation whose product are measured on the basis of quality of library services offers to a targeted community. The concept of differentiated marketing for libraries is to determine and set out to cater to more than one target group.

A library must consider different ways and means to reach its target group. It must think in terms of seeking differential advantage. It can make services/product advertised through various existing and latest techniques of marketing. Some of the internal and external promotional tools for LIS are as follows:

i) Oral presentations
ii) Demonstration diskettes
iii) Promotional film or video
iv) Leaflet or brochure
v) Telephones services
vi) Promotional mailing
vii) Computer network/LAN
viii) Internet
ix) Local advertising
x) Bulletin board
xi) Newsletter
xii) News release
xiii) Printed bookmark label
xiv) Library logo
xv) Seminars/Workshop
xvi) Exhibitions
xvii) CAS
xviii) SDI
xix) Acquisition list
xx) Reprography
xxi) Suggestion box
xxii) Posters and display
xxiii) Celebration of library week.

The widely-used method of promoting library services is the oral presentation which can be used both internally and externally supported by other promotional material. In small libraries personal contact is sufficient but in big libraries only personal contact is not enough, therefore other methods of promotional strategy should be adopted. The publicity value of selling information is twofold: First, if you give a good service, the word will spread, and your income will increase; second, you will show your colleagues that the service you provide is far from a drain on their budgets, but actually contributing to the overall income.

The following are some of the objectives of promotional strategy for LIS:

i) to create an awareness among target users of the existence and objectives of services.

ii) to attract more and more users through offering more and more competitive services.

iii) to educate current and potential users.

iv) to change for LIS.

v) to build a strong and positive image of the library.

vi) to introduce selling ideas.

The information requirement of library users are not static as information itself is not static because of its multidimensional growth, particularly after the induction of latest electronic mode. Therefore, to cater to the needs and expectations of users, community and to get know about their preference/priorities a continuous feedback system is required.

Libraries, instead of underestimating the reality and potentiality of user community's problems and grievances, must get in touch with a continuous process of feedback to have marketing objectives fulfilled. If the feedback system is flexible and open then changes for new adaption is expected and necessary in view of the entry of new information technology in

LIS. Therefore, the library must re-examine and rethink its basic services, target group, differential advantages, feedback system, users needs, marketing tools, P. R. programme and communication channel to provide a place for marketing of LIS so that a new image of library can be established. With the advent of electronic information there is a worldwide awakening of information and the library users have had raised hope for appropriate access points to serve their information needs. Libraries can take a good advantage from existing marketing strategies in an increasing competitive marketing situation. The initial market strategy for libraries is to identify if the current users could be encouraged to avail greater use of available library services.

Due to the rapid change in the scenario of constraints resources, cost inflation and competition, marketing has become necessary for libraries too. Increasing competition from commercial information suppliers has compelled librarians to consider implementing marketing techniques in their service.

For librarian marketing process, both users orientation and exchange relationship concepts need to be identified. The best library services will become meaningless until used by the right user at the right time. This marketing precept should be kept in mind while identifying the satisfying exchange relationship.

Library marketing consists of users and library activities and exchange relationship created through the creation, distribution, promotion and pricing, products, services, and ideas. Finance is the key to all activities which enables an individual and institution to set the priorities and achieve the goal accordingly. It is further observed that the present electronic era is largely influencing the corporate culture and the methods of working of the personnel including the librarians and the managers of information centres in India and abroad.

Interestingly, the librarians and the managers of information centres are also actively engaged to re-orient their efforts and implement information technology in their respective institutions depending upon the availability of resources at their disposal.

Under the electronic information era, the modernisation process requires a considerable amount of the investment of financial resource which is undoubtedly not within the easy reach of an organisation. It is further experienced that after the implementation of modernisation in a library or an information centre, the financial resources are still required for the procurement of books, journals, equipment, stationary items, furniture, computers, maintenance of systems and services and also meeting the other recurring and non-recurring essential expenditure.

With the advent of the electronic information era, the old concept of a library being only a storehouse of books has now changed. Consequently, in an academic organisation, a library is not only considered as a centre for the creation and recreation of information product and services, but also a dynamic catalyst of R&D activities having a strong role to contribute significantly for achieving academic excellence in an organisation. This fact has brought a major shift to the responsibilities of the libraries not only to engage to house the collection, and provide routine services to the end users but also to generate financial resources for their respective institutions.

This change has made a library as one of the important dynamic institutional organs like other department or centre with the capacity to generate financial resources. As a result, the image of librarians and the managers of information centres has automatically upgraded giving an opportunity to contribute financially to their respective institution through using available electronic information infrastructural resources and services. This has become more easy under the electronic information era as information is treated as the resource of resources, having multiplier effect on all developmental activities.

Information infrastructure plays an important role in the development and expansion of the facilities and services in an industrial society to a large extent. For this reason, government and the corporate world always give priority to promote the projects and initiatives for infrastructural development in all sectors. These days due to increased importance of information in the society, the present central government is also giving priority to finance infrastructural projects including the IT sector in the country. In this regard, various international tie-ups and collaborations are also being explored to seek adequate resources for the IT sector.

IT has an added advantage to contribute substantially to other activities in a society. The various components of IT are:

i) Computers.
ii) Telecommunications.
iii) Storage technologies.
iv) Databases.
v) Information systems.
vi) Microforms or micrographics.
vii) Expert systems.
viii) Videotext and teletext.

Computers are devices for automatically processing information. Computer instructions are put on as bits of information. Devices for storing information are classified as primary or secondary storage. Primary devices are LSI devices, i.e., memory chips, which are regarded as an integral part of the computer. Secondary devices are external components consisting of floppy discs or tapes.

Input device ⟶ CPU ⟶ Output device

Videotext and viewdata are (two-way) interactive systems for transmitting text or graphics stored in computer databases via the telephone network for display on a television screen. Teletext is a non-interactive (one-way) form of videotext, that is a method of transmitting text or graphics stored in a computer database, as a part of broadcast transmissions for display on a television screen. Videotext and teletext differ in the way they transmit the data and also in the way the user controls what data are to be displayed. Teletext's chief virtue is its ability to beam video images.

CD-ROM or Compact Disc Read Only Memory is a 12cm diameter disc made from polucarbonate substrate and a reflective metalised layer. A disc weighs 16 grammes. A typical CD-ROM can store about 650 MB data. One would get a better idea of the size of the data that a CD can hold if we say that a CD can hold about 2,50,000 pages of text of 5,000 handling systems and services. CD-ROM can store full motion video, animation graphic, text and high resolution audio. One should keep in mind that a floppy drive cannot run a CD. For running a CD one would require a CD drive. The time taken by a CD drive to find and grab a piece of information is known as access time. This is usually in milliseconds. The smaller the access time, the better the drive; the amount of data transferred from the CD-ROM to the computer in unit time is known as transfer rate.

Read Only Memory means that the information stored on a compact disc can only be read but it cannot be modified. As CD-ROM stores text, graphic or still images audio and video or moving images, one would need to install a sound card and speaker to enjoy the world of multimedia that a CD-ROM offers. The music (audio only) CDs were followed by CD-ROMs. CD-ROM can hold a variety of multimedia information. At one point of time, it was called CD-I or compact disc interactive. When read with a computerised reader, it responds intelligently to the user's instructions.

NETWORK TECHNOLOGIES IN MODERN LIBRARIES

Libraries are now busy in finding ways and means of exploiting the communication technology at their disposal to access their own and other library catalogues, CD-ROM databases and other resources. Some important communication and library networks established/under development in India are SIRNET, ERNET, I-NET, NICNET, INDONET, INFLIBENT, CALIBNET, MALIBNET, DELNET, etc. Computer networks are expected to play an increasingly important role in the libraries for resource sharing and management.

Networks are usually set up in such a way that groups or organisations that share some common goals communicate through computers and make use of each other's computer system and data. Each computer network has a host computer also known as a server, which is assigned the duty of controlling the complete network.

Computer networks have wide area communication facilities with following protocols such as Public Switched Telephone Network (PSTN) Public Data Network (PDN), Satellite Data Networks (SDN), Network of Leased Lines (NLL) and Integrated Service Digital Network (ISDN).

Presently many countries have set up dedicated Public Data Networks (PDN) for the data transfer, which works on a packet switched mode, wherein a physical line can be used more efficiently by multiplexing message packets from a number of sources. In the new electronic environment the role of information professionals is becoming challenging and crucial.

During the last decade, the internet has grown into a gigantic computer system allowing millions of computer users across the globe to access thousand of databases to retrieve or exchange the latest information on any topic conceivable in the world.

Gate Way Internet Access (GAIS) enables subscribers to log in to any database, send e-mail, read news, download files remotely run programmes on distant hosts and range of other applications. The global information structure consists of communication lines, communications satellites and linked-up computers in the form of internet that has enabled scientists and technologists, worldwide, to exchange their ideas and resources and keep themselves abreast with the latest developments in their respective field of activities.

Internet is a global collection of people and computers all linked together by many miles of cables and telephone lines, all able to communicate because they talk a common language, the Transmission Control Protocol/Internet Protocol (TCP/IP). Internet access by LIS staff will also facilitate them to provide better services by means of referral services, resource sharing, current awareness service, ordering of books, etc. Every library must plan for installing a web server at the library itself so that the right information will be provided to the users at the right time.

Library INTERNET Browsing Software (LIBS) is a Telnet-based network access tool that helps users to find a log-on to library catalogue systems. The system also grew in size, connecting to numerous online library catalogues as well as Campus Wide Information System (CWIS), information services and a variety of databases.

The libraries in the internet sites can be searched and browsed by using any popular web browsers such as Netscape, MS internet Explorer, etc. Intranet is an internal network that uses the internet standards of HTML (Hyper Text Mark-up Language) and HTTP (Hyper Text Transfer Protocol) and the TCP/IP communication protocol along with a graphical web browser to support business application and provide departmental, inter-departmental and organisation-wide communication solutions. For example, an internet can be as simple as an internal web server that allows employees access to an employee handbook and a phone list.

The Intranet on the floor below could include sophisticated interactions with a database, video conferencing, private discussion groups, and multimedia. Subscription rate of scientific periodicals and cost of books have been increased rapidly. A stage may well arrive when the library funds are not at all sufficient to meet these costs. The internet provides access to an enormous number of databases distributed around the world. It collectively offers tremendous potential for collaborating and for sharing resources such as, documents, software, data and network services.

With multimedia technology we have image libraries, audio libraries, and even digital video libraries. Traditional libraries budgets devote an ever-increasing share of their funds to electronic services, whether in the form of CD-ROM's, online public access catalogues, or online databases. A digital storage costs go down relative to cost of library shelf space, and as electronic services become more useful, affordable, available and usable, there is a move towards the grand challenge of a world digital library stream.

The L&I profession is passing through a nebulous metamorphosis, especially with regard to the technical medium in which libraries are now functioning. In essence, an overall intensification of specialisation both in the technological aspects of information retrieval work and stronger subject oriented competencies and evaluative abilities are being developed for information professionals.

The in-service training and continuing education should be intensified to meet the changing demands at the workplace. To sustain important services with fewer staff and resources and even developing new services to meet the new demands of clientele are more common in the libraries. The increased use of information super highway and its limitations present subject-oriented challenges to the practising library professionals. These affect not only the methods and devices used for information accessibility, acquisition and control but also the retrieval precision to provide the targeted information in the correct context.

The librarians and information workforce should be prepared to receive and keep pace with technological changes and face them boldly. One of the great challenges for an explorer on the internet is to find the information needed from the millions of resources available. Since no person or organisation is in charge of the internet, there is no master list of all its resources. Finding the data you want can be time-consuming. Thus, it is not surprising that enterprising adventures on the internet decide to make it easier for themselves by writing software to facilitate the hunt. India's present annual demand for paper is estimated at 35 lakh tons and the figure was expected to touch the 50 lakh ton mark by the year 2000. The paper mills in the country can produce only 17 lakh ton. So the computer is not enough. There should also be a computer culture and documents movement in the office should be on the system itself while messages can be sent on e-mail. Regarding development of IT and telecommunication networks, the information scenario is heading for paperless library which may involve:

i) Active promotion of LIS for optimising utilisation of resources and services.

ii) Designing and developing user-friendly online information systems and services to provide easy and multi-access to information.

iii) Adopting and evaluating the newly emerging information technologies to exploit their potential for effective processing, storage, retrieval and the dissemination of information.

iv) Developing a highly motivated, skilled and competent workforce to manage and operate effectively.

v) Libraries at local and nation level should form resource sharing groups under LAN and WAN for maximum utilisation of money, men, materials and to avoid unnecessary duplication.

vi) Induction of information technology in organised manner to ensure system compatibility, connectivity, monitoring and evaluation of the computerisation and networking programmes.

vii) Stimulate and promote an harmonious programme of human resource development to the changing needs of LIS.

viii) to promote technological installations like networking teletext, telex, fax, videotex, online access, CD-ROM, e-mail, and other for free access information.

DIGITAL LIBRARIES

A typical digital library is a media server connected to high speed networks. The dawn of information revolution is considered to be one of the marvels of the twentieth century. The new technology has not only transformed the shape of modem libraries but also created very many exciting possibilities and opportunities. With radio, television, computers, communication satellites, cable TV, multimedia, local and wide area networks we are often referred to be living in an 'Information Society'.

Unlike traditional libraries, digital libraries don't reside in a building. In addition to traditional text-based information data accessible through the digital library system includes non-text information (photographs, drawings, illustrations, work of art); streams of numeric data (satellite information, cosmological data); digitised sound and moving visual images and 3D representations (holograms). In the context of digital imaging, librarians face greater challenges in capturing, storing, formatting, retrieval and reproduction of non-textual information, because it is a new area of developing sources of information and experiences are few. The technical aspects of digital imaging are far beyond the scope of most of our libraries. As the arrival of digital libraries is imminent, librarians are forced to re-educate themselves to meet this new challenge.

The rapid technological developments as well as economic changes have made it clear that the familiar role of librarians as information intermediaries must undergo immense change, if the librarians are to avoid being displaced by a variety of contenders. The collections of libraries and archives, the primary repository of analog form of information constitute print (documents) image form (map and photographs) and sound formats (records and videotapes). In other words, the principal categories of information sources are text, video and voice. The visual representation of objects, colours and shapes has always been an integral part of human culture. Hence the representation of visual phenomena through photography, motion film and video have become part of our daily lives.

For information to be communicated broadly, it needs to be stored outside the human memory. Today, we have moved beyond text and language, into the storage and communication of images of this visual world. Now consider the imaging aspects of non-textual data. Looking back, recording of original non-textual (image) data was manual until the development of photography. The invention of silver-based film and photographic process added a new dimension to information acquisition, as it was possible to accurately capture complex visual images. Later on, electromagnetic media opened up new possibilities in capturing information through video tapes. Image information stored in these analog formats could not be processed easily and this led to the birth of magnetic and optical media.

Modern information systems are now able to represent the information electronically (as digital signals) and to manipulate automatically at high speeds. Such information represented digitally, in two states, or binary form is often referred to as digital information. Magnetic tapes (serial access), magnetic disks (direct access), and optical discs form the basic recording and storage media in digital forms. The capture of data for electronic storage and digital processing is accomplished by manual (keyboard) and automatic (image processing) techniques. Interestingly, it is observed that two-thirds of the information cannot be digitised by keyboard transcription because they contain drawings, signature, images, etc., or because keying-in would be highly uneconomical.

Digital Imaging

An image database seems a near perfect replacement for traditional methods of access, which require the handling of original non-textual formats. With numerous advantages it is clear that digital image databases will be used to a greater extent in the future. In the building of image, database includes phases such as scanning source material, interfacing the images with a database tool or delivering the images to the user. The power and attraction of digital image databases are attributed mainly to the synergy between the two complex technologies, namely, computerised search/retrieval system and digital imaging. Each of these disciplines—cataloguing on one hand, imaging science on the other hand—has long been a speciality of its own.

Image processing involves the use of high resolution scanning cameras. But how does a camera record and transform a 'document page' into a 'digital page' which can be read and manipulated by a computer? To generate a digital representation of a document page, cameras divide the page into minute areas called picture elements (pixels) and produce an array of binary digits, each representing the brightness of a pixel. The resulting stream of bits is enhanced, compressed and stored in high density storage media such as microfilm, PCMCIA card, optical discs, etc.

A document page of 2,500 characters require 45,000 bytes of space, while uncompressed. A PCMCIA card can hold up to 60-80 sharp but compressed pictures or document pages. These cards are reusable after loading the images on to computers and often erasing them. Digital cameras use special silicon chip incorporating electronic sensors such as Charged Couple Devices (CCD's).

The image scanner digitises the entire page into series of 'ones' and 'zeroes' and displays an image as it does not recognise characters and words of text. In other words, the scanner senses the presence of photons (light) rather than the electrical signals as in video cameras. After the picture is digitised the camera transforms it into one of the industry standard image file formats as per MPEG system or its equivalents such as TIFF, JPEG, EPS and DAVIC. The widespread deployment of digital technology is due to parallel advances in software which allow the technology to be used by persons other than computer experts.

To bring up the picture on to the monitor and to manipulate (cut, crop, reduce, brighten, soften, diffuse, twist, emboss, etc.) a host of software packages such as Photoplus, Photo finish, Image Assistant, etc., are available. These softwares do all these things in seconds that would have taken hours in the conventional wet process. This aspect is considered as the real strength of digital imaging.

Even though the principle of digital imaging is a decade old, digital cameras have emerged stronger, only in the recent three-four years. Industry leaders like Kodak and Canon and computer companies like Apple have found a new common ground. Digital cameras are available today with resolutions from 320 × 240 pixels to 4096 × 4096 pixels. An ordinary digital camera may cost between $1,000 and $5,000, but it may go up to $28,000 as in the case of NIKON N90 model, which runs high resolution (3060 × 2036 pixel) images. Nikon and Fuji have jointly developed SLR cameras which can record compressed as well as non-compressed data.

Data Compression

The concept of video compression is driven by many of the new applications in multimedia, image databases, video conferencing, interactive training, broadcast service, medical imaging and the national information infrastructure. Compressions means removing of unnecessary data such as spaces, which is restored when the data is decompressed.

According to Texas Instruments, transmitting uncompressed data require about 216 megabits per second (mbps) compared to 6 mbps required to send the same amount of data when compressed. Due to economic reasons, the bandwidth available in most of the networks is limited and this demands data to be compressed before it is transmitted across such a media. Any digital compression algorithm will normally have the capabilities, such as random access, audio, video and textual synchronisation, searchability, editability, scalability linked with network quality of service, asymmetric compression and security, and copyright protection.

There is an evolving shared vision of the new information world. It is defined as a world of ubiquitous, reasonably priced digital information in any and all media available to everyone from a computer, TV, palm or wrist, as predictable, ordinary and universal as a toaster. Technology has created a communality of approaches which is assumed to have led into the convergence, even across what has traditionally been a strongly-marked boundary. Experts feel that the adaptation of new technologies as a universal tool of information storage and retrieval has made it difficult and perhaps futile to attempt a fence around the information profession.

Compared to the analog form of graphic representation, digital imaging stands out as a wonder tool in the hands of the information technologists due to the following merits:

a) It permits direct and exact controls of numerous parameters, right on the monitor.

b) It has essentially abandoned film technology in document copying, colour reproduction, microfilm duplicating and graphic arts.

c) It produces detailed image information for immediate utilisation.

d) With one to three million pixel CCD's (charged couple devices) digital cameras provide high-quality pictures.

e) Digital reconstruction of faded photographs, maps, manuscripts and other library materials of archival value is much easier.

f) It is a powerful teaching tool; prototype could be presented by simulation which helps to visualise the actual process.

g) It has the capability to integrate different forms of data into a new form of representation.

The challenges facing by digital imaging technology are given below:

a) Digital imaging is not likely to replace conventional film-based methods completely.
b) The technology faces more difficulty with moving objects and this is being addressed constantly.
c) The reformatting projects in libraries currently involve high cost and labour.
d) Digital imaging consumes higher bandwidth which is limited in most of the networks. This factor restricts easy transport of data while networking.
e) Digital imaging emerged so quickly, that the technical and quality issues need to be addressed further.
f) It offers limited capabilities for demanding applications such as high speed, high resolution; and continuous tone imaging unlike in silver-based photographic systems.
g) The extent of usage of digital databases depends on the power of cataloguing/indexing system, which is still a concern.
h) The hardware and software becomes obsolete so fast that the preservation of digital images require a constant file refreshing and migration.
i) Digitised video consumes large quantities of computer power as each minute of digital video represents a large depository of data.
j) It is temporarily inhibited by cost, performance, user experience and supporting systems.

RESOURCE SHARING

Information is a very vital resource. It has been considered as a basic input. Overall development of a country depends largely on the volume of the knowledge it uses. It is required to support various activities related to planning, organising, policy making, and for decision-making function.

To provide pinpointed, expeditious and exhaustive information at the right time to the right person, it is essential to use modern information technology. Today it is beyond the working ability of any library to cater to and satisfy the information needs of the user without using modern information technology.

The aim of using information technology is encashing efficiency, improving reliability and reducing costs. Teaching and research in all the institutes are centred around their libraries.

The libraries with their limited financial resources, face serious problems in managing enormous information flow. It is essential for libraries to share their resources and organise services on a cooperative basis to satisfy collectively the information needs of users. The convergence of computer and communication technologies has expanded the horizons of the individual library to resources on a national scale.

The recent progress in telecommunication has been a major impetus to the development and expansion of library network. The network functions are:

i) To optimise collection in libraries with limited budget.
ii) To promote and support adoption of standards in library operations.
iii) To improve efficiency of housekeeping operations.
iv) To generate new services and to improve the efficiency of the existing services.

In the network environment inter-library loan is possible through electronic mail facility. The person at the other end reads the mail and locates the relevant document. If the document is available in machine-readable from, it will be sent through e-mail, otherwise the hard-copy will be sent through courier service. In online environment one can search the holding of the other library. If the documents are available, a message can also be made for sending it on loan. The acquisition system can be easily possible with the help of online ordering facility.

In developed countries online families enable the publishers and booksellers to link through networks. The libraries thus have access to latest information and can decide whether they should acquire a particular book. The sharing of cataloguing when the proofs of a book are at the printing stage are vital. The serial control is also possible in an integrated system. Nowadays as library automation and networks are growing the need for trained and skilled manpower also grows. It is essential that the expertise of the skilled personnel is shared. The union catalogue of all participating libraries of network should be compiled and updated regularly in science and technology.

As information is an important resource of the library, it can be shared through e-mail and networking, and is stored in machine-readable from. Some information networks services are: (1) MEDLIND-U.S. National Library of Medicine (2) IINFLIBNET (3) AGRIS and (4) DIS. Institutes like INSDOC provide translation services to scientists. They should create translation banks in machine-readable forms. To make information available through resource sharing networks, each library in the network should develop collection, specialising in the areas of their interest. It is achieved by arranging the deposit of publications at local and regional levels. It reduces duplication of material and provides more space for new books to the particular library. Resource sharing networks are available at local, regional national or international levels.

Today the information function stretches beyond the precincts of a library. It challenges all those engaged in the systematic organisation, processing and handling of information and data. There has been a remarkable boarding of an information requirement base. For a number of reasons there is reluctance to accept change. But there is a new outlook on the horizon which promises an appreciable degree of interaction which is beginning to take place between people working in different sectors. Areas in which cooperation is feasible are being actively sought and there is increasing evidence of attempts to undertake joint evaluation of new systems and techniques.

The impact of an electronic computer on library services is dramatic. The distance over which data can be transmitted ranges from a few metres to any place the world over. The machine has taken over all the routine work of selection, abstracting, indexing and cataloguing, previously done by professional information officers and libraries. The steadily growing range of commercially available subject-oriented current awareness services in hard copy forms has devalued the importance of in-house service.

As the computer capabilities has increased, more convenient to use, online access to information will be only a telephone connection away from him. Instead of calling the library for information the inquirer will be in a position to dial the appropriate file from his terminal. The economic benefits of resource sharing may be outlined as follows:

i) No library can afford to acquire all published materials in the areas of its specialisation, due to high procurement cost and investments on processing servicing, space and personnel.

ii) The application of new technology to resource sharing will ensure that useful information is made available to users effectively and fast; thus we can save valuable time of the users.

iii) Cooperative collection development can result in effective relationship between libraries.

iv) Shared cataloguing and classification through networking can reduce the financial burden on each library.

E-mail in Libraries

E-mail services offer new, fast and economic modes of information to its users. It connects the global information generators with each other to share their knowledge. The latest technology of e-mail provides tremendous opportunities for the users of libraries and information centres to deliver the information at the desktops of information seekers. Most of the services of the libraries can perform more easily through e-mail giving tremendous performance and productivity to satisfy their users.

E-mail services make the acquisition work quicker, accurate and easy. All the correspondence with booksellers and publishers can be done through e-mail. You may send supply orders, reminders for supply, and verify the prices from the publisher or distributor directly. You can get bibliographical details and download their catalogues. You can confirm the billing and their payments. E-mail services benefit academicians, ordinary information-seekers or miscellaneous groups by providing the right information at the right time.

FTP (File Transfer Protocol) and Archie

File Transfer Protocol (FTP) facilitates transfer of files over the internet. The complete process involves the transfer of file from one host to another. FTP has become popular and a most widely used tool because of the number of anonymous FTP servers available.

Archie is the companion software tool to FTP. The Archie programme reaches a constantly updated index of FTP sites, file names and descriptions. It helps us to find information located anywhere on the internet.

Telenet

Telenet delivers you to the front door of other networks. Through telenet we can browse library card catalogues, search for papers or journals of interest. Telenet allows one to log on to another system and use various services available on that host computer.

Usenet

Usenet allows us to send messages to a specific person or group. Network news lets one send messages on an electronic bulletin board for anyone to see. Both e-mails and news groups are extremely useful internet tools. Usenet newsgroups are the vast array of discussion groups located on the internet. Librarians may be reluctant to use such a source in order to answer reference questions, because answers to posts can come from anyone and there is no way to verify the authoritativeness of the answer received. However, some librarians have found Usenet useful for answering questions about popular culture as well as about specialised topics.

The best advice for using Usenet is to inform the patron before posting a query to Usenet that is the method being used to answer the question and to receive the patron's permission to do so. In addition, the patron should be informed that the answer(s) received may or may not be correct and that the librarian has no way of verifying the 'expertise' of the person(s) responding to the query. Thousands of newsgroups exist, and new ones appear every day.

Newsgroup articles are not the same kind of articles that we might find in a newspaper. These are discussion groups, classified as announcements, and just plain old bulletin-board services. But the topics are divided by groups. We can select one of interest to us. Group names are often three or more words long, separated by periods. The first word provides a very general description of the group, and each following word becomes more and more specific.

Gopher and Veronica

Gopher is a software tool that connects a variety of computers and information databases on the internet and displays them as a series of menu items. Gopher servers accept simple query and sends to the clients a document or a list of documents.

Veronica ("very common rodent-oriented network index to computerised archives") is the companion tool to gopher. It is a search tool that allows one to quickly scan gopher for particular files and directories. It is a programme that one can access through gopher.

World Wide Web (WWW)

The internet provides many opportunities for librarians to provide increased and more efficient service to patrons. Some ways of integrating the use of the WWW into reference are discussed here. First, a word for the 'authoritativeness' and reliability of information of the WWW (World Wide Web).

New information appears on the WWW at an astounding rate. Criteria for evaluating material on the WWW are similar to those we use to evaluate print or other electronic resources. Listservs are one of the most popular uses of the internet. They can be used to network with other librarians across the country, to share similar problems and to find out how other libraries are dealing with issues that we encounter in our library.

The aspect of creating a web page is to identify and utilise the potential of the Web as an alternative medium for delivering library services and for using library databases. After integrating the WWW into providing reference service, we may want to think about putting our library on the WWW and developing some of these innovative applications. Creating HTML documents is not difficult, but may be time consuming. However, the exposure and availability of reference resources through a web page can be a valuable service.

Community Networks

Community networks are being formed around the country to give residents better access to internet resources and to bring about a sense of local community. Public libraries have traditionally performed the role of being an information and retrieval organisation for the community. Libraries also have the opportunity to become public access sites, providing net access to patrons for free.

INFORMATION SECURITY POLICY

Policy formulation is an important step toward standardisation of security activities for IT resources. IT security policy is generally formulated from the input of many members of an organisation, including security officials, line managers, and IT resource specialists. However, the policy is ultimately approved and issued by the organisation's senior management. In environments where employees feel inundated with policies, directives, guidelines and procedures, an IT security policy should be introduced in a manner that ensures that management's unqualified support is clear. The organisation's policy is the management's vehicle for emphasising the commitment to IT security and making clear the expectations for employee involvement and accountability.

Formal IT security policy helps establish standards for IT resource protection by assigning programme management responsibilities and providing basic rules, guidelines, and definitions for everyone in the organisation. Policy thus helps prevent inconsistencies that can introduce risks, and policy serves as a basis for the enforcement of more detailed rules and procedures. Ideally, the policy will be sufficiently clear and comprehensive to be accepted and followed throughout the organisation yet flexible enough to accommodate a wide range of data, activities, and resources.

Two types of policy will typically need to be developed to meet an organisation's needs: programme-level and issue-specific. Programme-level policy's main function is to establish the security programme, assign programme management responsibilities, state the organisation-wide IT security goals and objectives, and provide a basis for enforcement. Issue-specific policies also need to be developed, in order to identify and define specific areas of concern and to state the organisation's position and expectations in relation to them.

Programme-level Policy

Programme-level policy is broad in scope and far-reaching in applicability. To make the subject more manageable, an effective approach to a discussion of programme-level IT security policy is to break general policy into its basic components: purpose, scope, goals, responsibilities, and enforcement. A primary purpose of programme-level policy is to establish the IT security programme. This includes defining the programme management structure, the reporting responsibilities, the roles of individuals and groups throughout the organisation, and the organisation-wide goals of the security programme. Additionally, the programme-level policy should serve the purpose of emphasising to all employees the importance of IT security and clarifying the individual employee's role and responsibilities.

The IT security policy may be met with a degree of scepticism unless given appropriate visibility and support by top management, and that visibility and support should be clearly and energetically reflected in the programme-level policy and in its emphasis on employee participation. The programme-level policy should thus firmly establish individual employee accountability. Employees should be made aware via the policy that even if they are not designated IT security programme personnel, they none the less have significant IT security responsibilities.

Programme-level policy should be of sufficient breadth of scope to include all of the organisation's IT resources, including facilities, hardware, software, information, and personnel. In some instances, it may be appropriate for a policy to name specific assets, such as major sites, installations, and large systems.

The three security-related needs universally most emphasised among IT resource experts and the general computer user community are integrity, availability, and confidentiality. These concepts are the focus of many discussions in this handbook as well. These concepts should be the basis of the goals established for an organisation in its IT security policy. Integrity means assuring that information is kept intact, and not lost, damaged, or modified in an authorised manner. Availability means assuring that information is accessible to authorised users when needed and that to the extent possible, IT systems are safe from accidental or intentional disablement. Confidentiality means assuring that information is accessible only as authorised and that it cannot be acquired by unauthorised personnel and/or via unauthorised means. Goals related to these concepts should be stated in meaningful ways to employees based on the given environment.

In an organisation responsible for maintaining large but not highly confidential databases, goals related to reduction in errors, data loss, or data corruption might be specifically stressed. In an organisation responsible for maintaining much more confidential data, however, goals might emphasise increased assurance against unauthorised disclosure. In addition to the security programme management responsibilities, many other responsibilities throughout the organisation should also be discussed in the policy, including the role of line managers, applications owners, data users, and the computer systems security group.

The relationships among various individuals and groups may also need to be defined in the programme-level policy. Such clarification can diminish ambiguity and confusion related to areas of responsibility or authority. It might be desirable to clarify, for example, who is to be responsible for approving the security measures to be used for new systems or components being installed: should it be the department line manager where the item will be installed? Or should it be a designated inter-departmental IT security specialist? It might even be desirable to indicate under what circumstances, if any, approval of security measures implemented would be warranted by the head of the security programme.

Programme-level policy serves as the basis for enforcement by describing penalties and disciplinary actions that can result from failure to comply with the organisation's IT security requirements. Discipline commensurate with levels and types of security infractions should be discussed. Consideration should also be given to the fact that non-conformance to policy can be unintentional on the part of employees.

Whereas the programme-level policy is intended to address the broadest aspects of IT security and the IT security programme framework, issue-specific policies need to be developed to address particular kinds of activities and, in some environments, particular systems. The types of subjects covered by issue-specific policies are areas of current relevance, concern, and, sometimes, controversy upon which the organisation needs to assert a position. In this manner, issue-specific IT security policies help to standardise activities and reduce the potential risks posed by inadequate and/or inappropriate treatment of the IT resources.

Issue-specific Policies

Issue-specific policies serve to provide guidelines for the further development of procedures and practices within the functional elements of an organisation. Programme-level policy is usually broad enough that it does not require much modification over time. Issue-specific policies are likely to require revision and updating from time to time, as changes in technology and related activities take place. This is largely because as new technologies develop, some issues diminish in importance while new ones continually appear.

A major challenge to IT security specialists has long been the fact that for every new technology there are also new associated problems and issues to be addressed. Many organisations today are developing and refining communications security policies in order to better address such questions as who should have e-mail access, how will privileges be assigned and monitored, for what types of activities and information is e-mail sufficiently secure, and what criteria should be used for the re-sending of messages among users. Another topic of recent notoriety impacting IT security policies is the threat posed by computer viruses.

New viruses and new methods of transmitting them are making it necessary that organisations develop policies regulating activities that were once performed freely, such as exchanging floppy discs among users, accessing electronic bulletin boards, and using shareware products. A useful approach is to first break issue-specific policy into its basic components: statement of an issue, statement of the organisation's position, applicability, roles and responsibilities, and points of contact. Thereafter, some of the areas that often require issue-specific policies will be covered.

In order to formulate a policy on an issue, the issue must first be defined, with any relevant terms, distinctions, and conditions delineated. For example, an organisation might want to develop an issue-specific policy on the use of foreign software. Foreign software might be defined to mean any software, whether applications or data, not approved, purchased, screened, managed, and owned by the organisation. Additionally, the applicable distinctions and conditions might then need to be included, for instance, for software privately owned by employees but approved for use at work and for software owned and used by other businesses under contract to the organisation.

Once the issue is stated and related terms and conditions delineated, the organisation's position or stance on the issue will need to be clearly stated. To continue the example of developing an issue-specific policy on the use of foreign software, this would mean stating whether use of foreign software as defined is strictly prohibited, whether or not there are further guidelines for approval and use, or whether case-by-case decisions will be rendered based on some defined criteria.

Issue-specific policies will also need to include statements of applicability. This means clarifying where, how, when, to whom, and to what a particular policy applies. For example, it could be that the hypothetical policy on foreign software is intended to apply only to the organisation's own on site resources and employees and is not to be applicable to contractor organisations with offices at other locations. Additionally, the policy's applicability to employees travelling among different sites and/or working at home who need to transport and use discs at multiple sites might need to be clarified.

The issue-specific policy on foreign software, for example, might include procedural guidelines for checking discs used by employees at home or at other locations. It might also state what the penalties would be for using unapproved foreign software on the organisation's IT systems. For any issue-specific policy, the appropriate individuals in the organisation to contact for further information, guidance, and enforcement should be indicated. For example, for some issues the point of contact might be a line manager; for other issues it might be a facility manager, technical support person, or system administrator.

Some of the areas in which management today needs to consider issue-specific IT security policies are covered in this section. These topics are intended to provide examples and serve as sources for ideas and analysis. Although many of these topics are standard to any discussion of IT security, an organisation would necessarily need to tailor its policies relating to them to meet its own unique needs.

The physical protection of and access to IT resources and facilities will generally need to be addressed in one or more specific policies. In organisations with extensive IT systems and equipment, this may mean developing policies that address such issues as who has access to what sites/locations; how often risks to installations are be analysed and by whom; what types of physical access controls and monitoring equipment are put in place; what responsibilities will be assigned to trained security officials and what activities and responsibilities will be required of all employees.

Depending on the types of activities being performed, the degree of data sensitivity to be encountered, and the sheer numbers of personnel, specific security policies related to personnel screening, requirements, hiring, training, evaluating, and firing may need to be developed and administered. It may be appropriate that a trained personnel security specialist initiate, review, approve, and perform all security-related personnel actions.

Communications security is a complex technical specialty unto itself. In organisations where day-to-day business relies on communicating routinely with remote locations, the security of the communications transmissions and lines is usually an issue that needs to be addressed by policy. Issues associated with the use of cryptography and its related options and procedures, the use of modems and dial-in lines, and precautions against wiretapping are just some of the potential issues to be addressed.

Administrative security as it applies to IT system management and oversight activities comprises many potential security policy issues. Included are such topics as input/output controls, training and awareness, security certification/ accreditation, incident reporting, system configurations and change controls, and system documentation.

Risk management involves assessing IT resources in terms of potential threats and vulnerabilities and planning the means for counteracting those identified risks. Issues that will need to be addressed by policies include how, by whom, and when the assessments should be performed; and what type of documentation should result.

Related to risk management, contingency planning means planning for the emergency actions to be taken in the event of damage, failure, and/or other disabling events that could occur to systems. Issues that need to be addressed by policies include determining which systems are most critical and therefore of highest priority in contingency planning; how the plans will be tested, how often, and by whom; and who will be responsible for approving the plans.

Policy Implementation

Policy implementation is a process. Policy cannot merely be pronounced by upper management in a one-time statement or directive with high expectations of its being readily accepted and acted upon. Rather, just as formulating and drafting policy involves a process, implementation similarly involves a process, which begins with the formal issuance of policy.

Especially high visibility should be afforded the formal issuance of IT security policy. This is due to a combination of factors, including the following:

a) Nearly all employees at all levels will in some way be affected;
b) Major organisational resources are being addressed;
c) Many new terms, procedures, and activities will be introduced.

Providing visibility through such avenues as management presentations, panel discussions, guest speakers, question/answer forums, and newsletters can be beneficial, as resources permit. Including IT security as a regular topic at staff meetings at all levels of the organisation can also be a helpful tactic. As an aspect of providing visibility for IT security policies, information should also be included regarding the applicable higher level directives and requirements to which the organisation is responding.

Policy Documentation

Once IT security policy has been approved and issued, it may be initially publicised through memorandums, presentations, staff meetings, or a variety of means. As soon as possible, though, it will also need to be incorporated into formal policy documentation as well. The process of documenting policies will usually require updating existing documentation as well as creating new documentation.

Existing documentation: IT security will need to be integrated into many existing activities and practices throughout many levels of the organisation. This integration will be facilitated by revising any existing applicable documentation to reflect new procedures, rules, and requirements. Included may be the modification of various existing documents, forms, and plans at all levels of the organisation to reflect the IT policy. For example, if IT equipment purchases and/or upgrades have been reviewed and approved based on documented criteria such as cost, productivity, maintainability, etc., then security considerations may need to be introduced into that criteria.

New documentation: Additionally, the development of many new documents, such as guidelines, standards, and procedures, may be required. This is often true in large organisations performing many different activities and having many levels of management. In such environments, different functional elements may have widely differing IT systems and needs to accommodate. It is therefore generally more practical, to the extent possible, to allow elements to tailor their implementations of policy to meet their unique needs. For example, organisations will want to issue policies to decrease the likelihood of data loss due to technology failures and/or operator errors.

A programme-level policy might state something to the effect that: 'It is the policy of the organisation to ensure against data loss due to accidents or mishaps.' In an area where extensive writing and editing of lengthy documents is performed, such as a word processing or technical publications unit, security documentation might be developed on saving work in-progress much more often than would usually be done, and/or utilising automatic 'save' features on IT systems and software. In a different type of functional area, however, where, for example, databases are maintained that do not undergo significant changes very often, the security documentation might focus on procedures for the database administrator to use in performing periodic (daily, weekly, etc.) back-ups of the system. Appropriate visibility should be afforded the IT security policy through all applicable documentation.

The more integral security policy is to all other aspects of daily routines, the more quickly the associated actions and practices will become natural to doing business. Ultimately, among the goals of policy are the assimilation of a common body of knowledge and values and the demonstration of appropriate corresponding behaviors. Those goals will be expedited by making the IT security policy integral to the organisation through all avenues.

There are a number of potential costs associated with developing and implementing IT security policies. In some environments, the major costs may be those incurred through the numerous administrative and management activities required for drafting, reviewing, disseminating, and publicising the policies. In some organisations, though, successful policy implementation may require additional staffing, training, and equipment.

FUTURE OF LIBRARY SECURITY

Libraries are facing security problems and varying degrees of personal and professional risks since their earliest beginnings. One could even look at attempts for security as an exercise in futility because all attempts to make any library completely crime-proof have met with failure. Modern technology does not merely promise to create or improve better sensors and alarms to protect library collections. Emergent technology may actually slam the door on potential criminals, rendering them incapable of achieving their goals while helping publicise thefts and alerting other libraries. One thing on which book thieves have normally relied is that libraries do not talk to one another or exchange information about missing materials, thieves caught in the act, and methodologies used by those who steal.

Advances in technology may actually serve to make both theft and mutilation of materials and violence in library buildings things of the past by the simple expedient of removing the building from the equation. But even if we can never hope for perfect library security in existing buildings, we can at least work conscientiously toward that goal. There is no clear winner in view. In the coming age of virtual libraries, the era of the smash-and-grab thief will be over for libraries, and the day of the clever, resourceful electronic thief will be upon us, supplanting one problem with a potentially greater one. But even in this imperfect age of library vulnerability, we're getting better at catching crooks, or at least making their nefarious tasks far more difficult.

As better security measures are implemented the crooks get smarter, too, inventing new and even more ingenious methods of ripping us off. Still, in the foreseeable future, libraries might just have a few tricks up their sleeves to help them in this struggle against theft and pilferage. Subliminal programming, understandably a highly controversial issue, is based on the theory that the unconscious mind can absorb information that is imperceptible to the conscious mind. This effect can supposedly be achieved by flashing messages so fast that the eye cannot catch them or by playing soft audio messages that the conscious mind does not hear. Such messages are intended to communicate directly with the subconscious.

A subliminal message interrupts the television programme at random intervals just long enough to flash its text on the screen for one-thirtieth of a second. At that speed, the conscious human mind is numb to the intrusion. That speed may be too fast for the human eye to register, but, apparently, not so fast that the mind doesn't register its presence. The only presupposition is that the viewer is watching intently and concentrating. Looking down or away will, of course, defeat the whole purpose of the subliminal exercise

The developers of the subliminal weight-loss home system claim without hesitation that their programmes do not pose any serious psychological danger to most people, since TV viewers naturally filter out painful or unpleasant messages. Detractors, however, view this new technology with alarm. Who knows whether, in some subjects, the ostensibly harmless message could trigger involuntary reactions causing serious psychological repercussions of unknowable intensity and eventual impact? But let's put aside our qualms for a moment and consider the potential benefits of such technology for a library striving to hold onto its books and other property.

Suppose a library administration, fed up with the continual shrinkage of the collection of materials, decided to give a variation of this idea a try. It would be interesting to see whether the rate of book theft and other unexplained losses would drop and by how much after the institution of such programming. But there is a serious privacy issue involved here, since subliminal messages are invasive, and no one likes finding out that someone else has programmed such a message. If a library began pumping subliminal messages into the heads of unsuspecting patrons, it would only be implemented consistent with certain safeguards.

Emerging technology is providing some very interesting ways of identifying people by using factors as diverse as voice recognition, heartbeat, retinal structure, and even body odour. Authentication of identity relied on such methods as personal signatures, driver's license photographs, credit cards, and office keys. But all of these have been shown to be unreliable, granting unscrupulous persons access to untold proprietary collections and similar electronic mines of guarded information.

The advent of the virtual library may be the most significant change in the nature of the library. Libraries without walls, containing books without pages, are now broadly available on the internet, and more paperless books are coming all the time. Such a capability makes it possible for users to consult a library's catalogue and use or purchase books without ever setting foot in the building or even travelling to the host city. Digital books in virtual libraries, in fact, may be vulnerable to destruction or alteration—intentional or accidental—from a power surge, a lightning strike, or acts of sabotage.

The fragility of digital files, in fact, is of great concern to libraries, since more and more of them rely on silicon storage to hold and archive their materials and to make them more accessible without the risk of loss. Loss and the problem of paper deterioration make computer storage attractive as a medium of retention and distribution. The promise of electronic libraries is alluring and seductive for librarians up to their necks in crumbling print and hard copy information.

A power failure in an electronic library renders even the most powerful computers into mere paperweights, and even the largest store of information inaccessible. Then there is technological obsolescence. Today's state-of-the-art computer programme is very likely to be tomorrow's unusable document, what with the rapid and accelerating pace of technological progress. Information itself is becoming more fragile: ordinary type can withstand everything except destruction of the page on which it is printed, but it takes only a stray magnetic field or power surge to kill an electronic file forever. To this end, some malevolent people spend an inordinate amount of their time working up viruses that will spoil or erase other people's files.

Whatever the cause of the disruption, every library has to address the question of converting to electronic storage and delivery and solve the problem of what to do when the power goes off. This is not to be construed as an indictment of the rush of those libraries that can afford it to automate their holdings. It is only a warning that not all change is progress, and that not all progress is forward.

The dilemma of how to preserve and protect electronic documents while carefully observing all provisions of the copyright law continues, and will continue into the discernible future. Keeping their heads up and their eyes open may well, in fact, be the best way librarians can keep a reasonable level of security in library buildings. Security forces help, too, especially trained professionals who know their jobs well. And developing technology has provided and will continue to provide ways that we can safeguard our collections and assure the safety of people in our library buildings.

Imagine a virtual library in which the library's holdings are electronic, consisting of magnetised documents available to users by means of telecommunications and computer equipment. The risk of losing materials in the customary way—things lost to mildew, wear, vandalism, or walking out the door concealed on the persons or in the belongings of patrons—becomes a non-factor. The archival copy of each document could be held in a secure, remote location, unvisited and untouchable by users, and preferably backed up by additional copies held in other sites, safe against the possibility of fire, sabotage, lightning strikes, or other catastrophes. Under these circumstances, the matter of library theft becomes a non-issue because users never really hold original copies in their hands.

Imaging means that access to information is widely available and that there is literally nothing to steal. Nothing we would know or recognise as books, periodical issues, or works of art would have to be entrusted to users, which would protect the materials against loss or damage due to casual neglect or intentional malfeasance. For definitional purposes, imaging is the application of digital technology to the management and manipulation of information in non-digital formats such as paper, photographs, microforms, or voice. By scanning or frame-grabbing images of correspondence, maps, charts, or drawings are converted into digital files which are sent to a computer's central processing unit.

Scanned images appear on the computer's monitor. Although high-resolution monitors are desirable for viewing and acting upon one or two complete page images at a time, low-cost monitors can be used effectively to view partial pages. Libraries exist both to provide access to information and to preserve information, but these two goals have in the past often been at cross-purposes.

Previously, libraries favoured tight security for their rare and irreplaceable documents, requiring that they be used only with stringent restrictions, the most user-unfriendly being that they did not circulate. Today, with imaging technology, it is possible to hold in your hands a copy of the most unique and fragile archival document, without causing anyone the slightest anxiety about how you treat it or where it eventually ends up.

A document preserved in digital format can be reproduced endlessly, and even laser-printed and made available to patrons for a nominal charge. This eliminates the demand for photocopies, which must usually be refused because of the potential for damage. Allowing patrons to take home copies of previously restricted documents will eliminate at least one motivation to steal materials. Moreover, digitisation makes possible sending copies to scholars and users continents away.

High-quality imaging can create copies nearly indistinguishable from the originals of rare, expensive, and fragile materials that otherwise would not circulate. There is no need for patrons to see or hold the original documents, which can be kept under safe and optimal conditions in archival storage. Therefore, and paradoxically, even while it permits library-like usage, imaging will eventually eliminate the need for security for iibrary materials because scholars will work with high-quality facsimiles instead of originals. Another real advantage of imaging is automatically generated backup copies of each archived document.

For security purposes, duplicate copies of each disk can be made and stored off-site. At this point, the library may actually discard digitised paper documents. It is astonishing that, with imaging, reproductive fidelity is sometimes even better than the original documents, because scanners are not sensitive to wrinkles or tears in paper, and faint images are vastly improved by scanning. Even glossy photographs can be replicated with acceptable fidelity through laser and video printing. This is a major advantage of imaging over microfilm. Not everything connected with information provision would be completely secure, however, even if imaging became cheap, reliable, and pervasive.

Still vulnerable to theft would be the computer equipment and software used by the system. But even these things would be unstealable in the physical sense if the system were truly virtual and everyone accessed libraries from home. So as libraries move slowly but probably inexorably in the direction of virtuality and home access, the good news is that theft is likely to become a non-issue. The best news for all concerned, however, is that librarians who convert their holdings to electronic format will be able, by using imaging technology, to secure the safety of their data and original documents while at the same time creating substantially greater opportunities for using the information contained therein.

Document imaging technology boasts several advantages for use in libraries and archives as well. There is, of course, a corresponding list of common drawbacks and objections to imaging a library's collection which must be addressed in all fairness. Whatever the merits and drawbacks of imaging collections it is highly likely that the availability of images of archival documents will generate substantially greater usage of archive centres while the original documents will be secure from theft or damage resulting from that usage.

In the future, library security will become a field ripe for experimentation. Assuming that the goal of library provision will still be access to information, it makes sense to seek to improve security at the same time as we strive to enhance and maintain free access.

Bibliography

Arms, Caroline, *Campus Strategies for Libraries and Electronic Information*, Bedford, Mass., Digital Press, 1990.

Barnard, P., 'Cognitive Resources and the Learning of Human-Computer Dialogues', in Carroll, J. M. (ed.), *Interfacing Thought; Cognitive Aspects of Human-Computer Interaction*, Cambridge, Massachusetts, MIT Press, 1987.

Bennett, John L., 'Observations on Meeting Usability Goals for software products', *Behaviour and Information Technology*, 5, (2), 1986.

Beck, L.L., *A Security Mechanism for Statistical Database*, Dept. of Computer Science, Southern Methodist University, 1979.

Bjorn-Anderson, N. and Numford, E. (eds)., *Information Society*, North-Holland, 1982.

Brindley, L.J. (ed.), 'The Electronic Campus: An Information Strategy', *Library and Information Research Report 73*, London, British Library, 1989.

Chan, Lois Mai, 'Library of Congress Classification as an On-line Retrieval Tool: Potential and limitations', *Information Technology and Libraries* 5 (September), 1986.

Chin, F.Y., *Security in Statistical Databases for Queries with Small Counts*, ACM Trans, Database syst. 3(1): 92, 1978.

Computer-Based National Information Systems: Technology and Public Policy Issues, Office of Technology Assessment, US Congress, Washington, DC, 1981.

Daniel, Evelyn, 'Information Resources and Organisational Structure', *Journal of the American Society for Information Science*, 1983.

Davida, G., *et al., Security of Statistical Databases*, TR-CS-76-14, Dept.of EECS, University of Wisconsin, Milmaukee, 1976.

Denning, D.E., 'Are Statistical Database Secure?' *Tech. Report, Computer Science*', Dept., Purdue University, 1977.

Davida, G.I., Wells, D.L., and Kam, J.B., 'Security and Privacy', *Proceedings of IEEE 2nd International Conf. on Computer Software and Applications*, 1978.

Date, C. J., *An Introduction to Database Systems*, Addison Wesley, 1977.

Denning, D. E., 'Are Statistical Databases Secure? *Tech. Report, Computer Science*, Dept., Purdue University, 1977.

__________ and Schwartz, M.D., *The Tracker: A Threat to Statistical Database Security*, ACM Trans. Database Syst. *4*(1): 76, 1979.

DeMillo, R. A., and Dobkin, D., 'Recent Progress in Secure Computation', *Proceedings of IEEE 2nd International Conference on Computer Software and Applications*, 1978.

Dobkin, D., Jones, A. K., and Lipton, R. J., *Secure Databases: Protection against User Inference*, ACM Trans. Database Syst. *4*(1): 97, 1979.

__________, R. J., and Reiss, S. P., 'Aspects of the Database Security Problem', *Proceedings on a Conference on Theoretical Computer Science*, Waterloo, Canada, 1977.

Davida, G., *et al*., *Security of Statistical Databases*, TR-CS-76-14, Dept. of EECS, University of Wisconsin, Milwaukee, 1976.

__________, Wells, D. L., and Kam, J. B., 'Security and Privacy', *Proceedings of IEEE 2nd International Conf. on Computer Software and Applications*, 1978.

Fellegi, I. P., *On the Question of Statistical Confidentiality*, J Am. Statist. Assoc. *67*(337): 7, 1972.

______________, and Phillips, J. L., *Statistical Confidentiality: Some Theory and Applications to Data Dissemination*, Ann. Econ. Social Measurement *3*(2): 399, 1972.

Hansen, M.H., *Insuring Confidentiality of Individual Records in Data Storage and Retrieval for Statistical Purposes,* Proc. AFIPS FJCC, 39: 519, 1971.

Haq, M., 'Security in a Statistical Database', *Proc. Am. Information Sci. 11*: 33, 1974.

______________, 'Insuring Individual's Privacy from Statistical Database Users'. *Proc. AFIPS NCC* 14:941, 1975.

Hammer, M. M., and Mcleod, D. J., 'Semantic Integrity in a Relational Database System', *Proceedings of VLDB,* 1975.

Hansen, M. H., Insuring Confidentiality of Individual Records in Data Storage and Retrieval for Statistical Purposes. Proc. AFIPS FJCC, *39*: 519, 1971.

______________, Modern Methods for Computer Security and Privacy. Prentice-Hall, 1977.

Information Technology and Libraries. (Vols. 1) Chicago: Library and Information Technology Association, American Library Association, 1982.

Nargundkar, M. S., and Saveland, W., 'Random Rounding to Prevent Statistical Disclosure'. *Proc. Am. Stat. Assoc. Soc. Stat. Sec.*, 1972.

Raitt, David, (ed.), *Libraries for the New Millennium Implication for Managers*, London, Library Association Publishing, 1987.

Sharma, S.K., *Computer Networks for Library Development in Preparing Libraries for the 21st Century*, Delhi, ILA, 1995.

The Spreading Danger of Computer Crime, *Business Week*, April 20, 1981.

Weizenbaum, Joseph, *Computer Power and Human Reason*, W. H. Freeman, 1976.

Whisler, Thomas, *The Impact of Computer on Organisation*, Praeger, 1970.

Wood Michael, *Introducing Computer Insecurity* NCC, Manchester, England and John Wiley, New York, 1983.

Index